"As we dive into the creative and artistic potential of dreams, we discover a deeper sense of identity. For people new to dreams or life-long dream journalists, this book teaches us how to explore their 'existential meaning' using art, storytelling, ceremony, and treasure boxes. With examples and illustrations, this book provides a rich source of inspiration and makes dream discovery a fun and playful endeavor."

—**Laurel Clark, DD, DM,** *past president of the International Association for the Study of Dreams, author of* Intuitive Dreaming. *www.laurelclark.com.*

"Hamel's fascinating book demonstrates that the initiatory images and symbols provided by our dreams are essential to the psyche, as they support our passage from one life-stage to another. The author supplies concrete tools that will allow readers to progress autonomously into the future, with artistry, imagination and greater awareness."

—**Vera Heller, PhD,** *art therapy professor, Université du Québec en Abitibi-Témiscamingue (UQAT)*

"If you only remember one dream you can start a fruitful conversation with Psyche. When you have lifelong dream journals as a treasure chest available, you can foster a compassionate relationship with your inner self and inner artist. Dr. Hamel, a devoted dreamer and art therapist, shares how to tell the story of your dream life, offering a variety of creative and art-therapeutic methods that support a meaningful journey to your soul."

—**Mag. Johanna Vedral,** *psychologist, art therapist, and collage artist, author of* Collage Dream Writing, *teacher of creative writing. https://schreibstudio.at/*

Dreams and Nightmares in Art Therapy

Dreams and Nightmares in Art Therapy draws on the author's extensive art psychotherapy practice and teaching to provide a wide range of creative writing and visual art methods for dreamwork.

Blending theories such as Gestalt therapy and Jungian psychology with clinical examples from Dr. Hamel's own clients, this unique book offers an array of art therapy and other creative dreamwork methods, covering a large variety of media such as mask making, clay, collage, sandtray and painting. The author also presents seven different types of nightmares and introduces a simple and efficient five-steps art therapy method for reducing their intensity and their frequency. The book concludes with a unique synthesis of 11 dreamwork methods to draw wisdom from dream journals accumulated over a long period of time.

This book is ideal for anyone interested in developing a personal or professional practice using dream art therapy. The methods presented here will captivate readers with their originality and provide inspiration for all kinds of psychological, artistic and spiritual development.

Johanne Hamel, DPs, psychologist and art psychotherapist, specializes in dreamwork and in somatic art therapy. She has been teaching art therapy for 20 years at the Université du Québec en Abitibi-Témiscamingue and is currently an international lecturer in Thailand, the USA and Europe. More information can be found on her website *johannehamel.com*.

Hélène Hamel is a self-employed translator who holds an honor degree in translation and has been working mainly from English to French for more than 30 years.

Dreams and Nightmares in Art Therapy

The Dream of the Jaguar

Johanne Hamel

Translated by Hélène Hamel

Routledge
Taylor & Francis Group

NEW YORK AND LONDON

First published 2022
by Routledge
605 Third Avenue, New York, NY 10158

and by Routledge
2 Park Square, Milton Park, Abingdon, Oxon, OX14 4RN

Routledge is an imprint of the Taylor & Francis Group, an informa business

Library of Congress Cataloging-in-Publication Data

Names: Hamel, Johanne, 1952– author.
Title: Dreams and nightmares in art therapy : the dream of the jaguar / Johanne Hamel ; translated by Hélène Hamel.
Other titles: Rêves, art-thérapie et guérison, de l'autre côté du miroir. English
Description: New York : Routledge, 2021. | Includes bibliographical references and index. |
Identifiers: LCCN 2021007154 (print) | LCCN 2021007155 (ebook) | ISBN 9780367644611 (hardback) | ISBN 9780367644604 (paperback) | ISBN 9781003124610 (ebook)
Subjects: LCSH: Dreams—Therapeutic use. | Art therapy. | Self-actualization (Psychology)
Classification: LCC RC489.D74 H3713 2021 (print) | LCC RC489.D74 (ebook) | DDC 616.89/1656—dc23
LC record available at https://lccn.loc.gov/2021007154
LC ebook record available at https://lccn.loc.gov/2021007155

ISBN: 978-0-367-64461-1 (hbk)
ISBN: 978-0-367-64460-4 (pbk)
ISBN: 978-1-003-12461-0 (ebk)

DOI: 10.4324/9781003124610

Typeset in Times New Roman
by Apex CoVantage, LLC

This book is dedicated to all my art psychotherapy clients and art therapy students who worked on their dreams through all these years and thus helped me develop efficient methods to understand their existential messages. You made this book possible.

Contents

4   Lifelong Dream Journals Methods

Figures

About the Author

Johanne Hamel, DPs, psychologist and art psychotherapist, specializes in dreamwork and art therapy as well as in somatic art therapy. She has been teaching art therapy for 20 years at the Université du Québec en Abitibi-Témiscamingue, Québec, Canada. She is the author of Art Therapy, Dreams and Healing: Beyond the Looking Glass, published at Routledge in 2021. She also published three books on art therapy in French, including a co-authored book on art therapy through Larousse, Paris. She is currently an international lecturer at the International Program of Art Therapy in Thailand (IPATT), at the International Association for the Study of Dreams (IASD) in the USA and for the European Consortium for Art Therapies Education (ECArTE), among others. She maintains a private practice in Sherbrooke, Québec, Canada.

Note on the translator:

Hélène Hamel is a self-employed translator who holds an honor degree in translation and has been working mainly from English to French for more than 30 years.

Foreword

Dreams can inspire us, guide us and help us discover hidden treasures within our own psyches. Although we might describe a dream in words, the dream expresses itself in images, symbols and feelings. Some dreams speak to us with music and movement. Exploring their visual elements, using active imagination and identifying a "felt sense", we can connect with spiritual and intuitive knowledge that lies beyond our conscious waking awareness.

As we dive into the creative and artistic potential of dreams, we seem to discover a deeper sense of identity, a more real understanding of who we are as spiritual or soulful beings.

For people new to dreams or those who have kept a lifetime of dream journals this book teaches us how to investigate the "existential meaning" of our dreams; in other words, what they reveal to us about ourselves, our attitudes, our feelings and our participation in the events and relationships in waking life. Dr. Hamel describes how to view our dream journals as a spiritual autobiography, noting patterns and connections like threads woven into the fabric of our lives.

One of my favorite parts of this book is Chapter 4, which describes 11 ways to examine our lifelong dream journals using visual art, three-dimensional art, storytelling, ceremony, treasure boxes and other creative methods. With examples and illustrations, this provides a rich source of inspiration and makes dream discovery a fun and playful endeavor.

As a life-long dreamer, I always look forward to learning new ways to reflect on my dreams. In my experience, dreamwork is most fulfilling when I discover something new about myself, something that was previously unknown. I appreciate this book because it can be used for self-study, with a dream partner or a group, to plumb the depths of a dream for self-revelation and illumination.

Dr. Johanne Hamel is uniquely qualified to show us how to tap into the creative potential of our dreams. An artist, psychologist and art psychotherapist, Dr. Hamel gives examples from her own dreams as well as her clients to lead us to greater understanding. This makes it an easy-to-use guide for those working with their own dreams, for parents who want to help their children, and for psychologists and therapists with their clients.

Dr. Hamel provides references for scholars who want to further research the sources she quotes but the writing is clear for a layperson as well.

This is a book I will keep in my toolbox of dream resources. I can imagine coming back to it at different times for new perspectives on my dreams. Like a dream which has many layers of significance, this seems to be a book with many applications for dreamers at all levels of experience.

I hope you enjoy playing with your dreams and exploring your creativity. May this lovely companion bring you insight on your journey to self-discovery.

Laurel Clark, DD, DM, is a teacher of metaphysics, certified dreamologist, intuitive counselor, interfaith minister, past president of the International Association for the Study of Dreams, and author of *Intuitive Dreaming*. In her spare time she plays with color as an abstract artist. For more information, see www. laurelclark.com.

Preface

The Dream of the Jaguar: Why this Mysterious Subtitle?

This subtitle refers to the strangest experience I have ever had with dreams, about 15 years ago, an experience I never forgot. You will find this story in Chapter 4, where I explain how we can explore our *dream animals*. This brings us very close to shamanic traditions of working with *power animals*. Dr. Alberto Villoldo, a psychologist and medical anthropologist, talks about the traditions of the Laikas, an aboriginal tribe from South America, in many of his books (2018, 2007, 2006a, 2000). The Laikas have four animals that are particularly important to their culture. They each represent an essential life principle, and together they offer a four-step approach to healing and growth: the snake, the jaguar, the hummingbird and the eagle (Villoldo, 2007, 2006a, 2000).

For the Laikas, the jaguar symbolizes the second stage of this healing process. It guides us to explore the darkest inner places we are afraid to visit. The jaguar essentially represents powerful self-transformation of our beliefs, ideas and emotions; it helps us understand that life crises are opportunities to let go of a pattern, to experience a process of death and rebirth (Villoldo, 2018, 2007, 2006a, 2000).

This is similar to what dreams enable us to do for ourselves: the artistic reproduction of a dream animal guides us to an existential message relevant to our life. I believe the symbol of the *jaguar* is a particularly meaningful way to represent the journey we undertake deep within ourselves when we work with our dreams. Over the years, I have found the sacred and spiritual aspect of this self-transformation work to be more and more powerful and essential. It is the *royal way towards the Self* which, according to Carl Jung (1991), is the spiritual and central part of the psyche.

This book introduces essential knowledge of the science of dreamwork and teaches art therapy and creativity methods to help clarify existential messages to be found in dreams. As I have had a much-diversified dream art therapy practice for over 35 years, I am offering a large variety of methods, all that I have explored that support so beautifully this deep and meaningful journey into our soul.

Art therapists, psychologists, psychotherapists and the general public still know little about the worlds of dreams and art therapy, and the possibilities they offer for personal transformation and growth. Yet dream psychotherapy is extremely effective; it brings us directly to the core of the psyche, especially when it invites the image and the symbol to complement the verbal exploration of dreams. I hope this book will enable everyone to grasp the richness of the therapeutic work of the *way of the dream*[1] and of the methods of creativity and art-therapy that exist to facilitate this work.

Johanne Hamel, D. Ps.

Note

1. A reference to the wonderful book by Boa, F. (1994). *The way of the dream: Conversations on Jungian dream interpretation with Marie-Louise von Franz*. Boston and London: Shambhala.

Acknowledgments

I am very grateful to everyone who so enthusiastically and generously contributed theirs dreams to this book and experimented with the creative and art therapy methods: Aimée-Édith, Andrée, Brigitte, Carole, Catherine, Édith, Emmanuelle, Francine, Françoise, Janeth, Jessica, José, Lise, Madeleine, Mario, Murielle, Sonia and Théo.

A special thank you to Marie-Johanne Lacroix, writer, for her participation in exploring collage and to France Raymond d'Aragon for her experimentation of the *four-steps method*. Thank you to art therapists Francine Duguay, for her *dream mantis/shield*, Françoise Pelletier for her dream *jaguar woman*, as well as to Madeleine Lévesque and to Emmanuelle Dupuis.

Thank you to Édith Bergeron, psycho-educator, for her example of an intervention with a 5 year old child and to Lise Pouliot, school psychologist who, with Édith Bergeron, commented my *Guide for Parents and for Child Therapists: How to Deal with Night Terrors and Nightmares in Children and Toddlers*.

Thank you also to Céline Tardif, art therapist, who contributed to this book with her comments on the content and for her help in putting this book together and to Sophie Boudrias, psychologist and art therapist, for her contribution on Haïkus. Thank you to Alexandra Duchastel, psychologist and art psychotherapist, for her precious rituals.

Thank you to Murielle Angers-Turpin and Maria Ricardi, art therapy teachers at the Université du Québec in Abitibi-Témiscamingue, who suggested to some students in their classes to experiment with some of my methods. Thank you to two students in their classes who generously agreed to participate in this project by providing their own examples of dreamwork.

Thank you to Hélène Hamel, who put a lot of energy into translating this book very seriously and professionally and to André Carrière, who generously offered a proof-reading!

And last but not least, my most heartfelt gratitude to Laurel Clark, DD, DM, teacher of metaphysics, certified dreamologist, intuitive counselor, interfaith minister, past president of the International Association for the Study of Dreams, author of *Intuitive Dreaming* and abstract artist, who warmly accepted to write the Foreword of this book.

Introduction

As Gayle Delaney said, *Dreams can provide some of the most beautiful and inspirational experiences of your life* (1996, p. 208). Having intimately experienced and witnessed this phenomenon, we are pleased to present this book intended for everyone who would like to explore themselves through dreamwork. Art therapists, psychologists and psychotherapists who are interested in becoming more knowledgeable about the widest range of creative and art therapeutic approaches involving dreamwork will find treasures herein. The methods presented primarily use writing and visual arts and are very likely to provide *inspirational experiences,* even though the primary purpose of art therapy dreamwork is not aesthetic in itself, as you will see in the artworks created from the dreams described in this book. Indeed, it is by no means necessary to know how to paint, draw or sculpt to take advantage of art therapy dreamwork. The methods proposed in this book are mostly inspired by the Gestalt and Jungian approaches in psychology. The perspective is actually humanistic and values human subjectivity. We strongly believe that only the dreamer is capable of identifying the true meaning of his dreams, and that art and creativity are the most efficient means to project and perceive the depth of one's individual reality. But as Jung insisted, "Plastic arts activity alone is not enough. Any evolution process requires an intellectual and emotional understanding of what is represented in order to allow integration into consciousness, both rationally and morally" (1993, p. 126)[1].

In my first book on dreams entitled *Dreams, art therapy and healing – Beyond the looking glass (Rêves, art-thérapie et guérison. De l'autre côté du miroir),* published for the first time in French more than 25 years ago, four basic art therapeutic approaches were presented, in addition to brief methods and experiential approaches. However, since then I have explored a much broader range of methods using all kinds of artistic mediums. Some of the writing approaches presented in this book are mentioned in various forms in the most popular books on dreams, while others cannot be found anywhere else, especially the art therapy methods. The purpose of this book is to illustrate the whole range of creative approaches available and a large number of art therapy methods. The clinical examples are taken for the most part from my own art psychotherapy practice.

DOI: 10.4324/9781003124610-1

The purpose of the approaches presented is always to help the dreamer find the *existential message* of his dreams as easily and efficiently as possible. While creative methods are both quicker and less inclusive, they often enable the dreamer to successfully identify the existential message. On the other hand, art therapeutic methods require using more extensive mediums in visual arts, which by themselves have a significant psychological impact. In all instances, the ultimate goal of any dreamwork remains to find the existential message, because this is the best way to help the dreamer efficiently manage his inner world and day-to-day reality. After all, as Jung said, "Because dreams are the most common and most normal expression of the unconscious psyche, they provide the richest material for its investigation" (1993, p. 71).[2]

In this book, the dreamer will learn how to do this by using the extraordinary potential of creative writing, images and artistic mediums.

The Dream's Existential Message

I should point out that grasping *the dream's existential message* means perceiving in our deepest self and beyond any doubt what our dream uncovers about the way we experience human existence. This involves re-entering the dream realm and allowing ourselves to be moved by what the dream's images and symbols seek to reveal. Ultimately, the dreamer is the only one to understand the existential message carried by his dream, because he is the only one able to assess if the message reflects clearly his feelings and the images present in his dream.

Grasping the dream's existential message gives us a chance to explore deeper sides of our life experience as well as feelings that might have been just vaguely apprehended or totally unconscious until then, which in turn leads to a totally new perception of ourselves and to a spectrum of possibilities never considered before. We come out of this with a renewed, deeper and profoundly gratifying relationship with ourselves and a broader self-awareness. Our inner world is consequently enriched with experiences and unexplored potentials. It unveils itself through our dreams, our imagination and through art. The approaches proposed in this book offer many gateways to this inner realm.

We can identify the existential message by asking ourselves what we are left with after having explored a dream through artwork and creativity or what the dream *viewed as a whole* is revealing or teaching about ourselves. The *primordial image* is often a good start for exploring a dream.

The dream's primordial image is the one that sticks in our mind when thinking back to a dream; it is usually the most vivid one for us. While remembering a dream, there is usually a specific image that keeps coming back and this is what I call the dream's primordial image.

The elucidation of the dream's message resides in what we *felt* while exploring the dream, in what stirred a reaction in us, whether positive or negative; it does not necessarily have to do with the *meaning* automatically given to the dream. After dreamwork, if many existential messages come to your mind, seek the most holistic one that encompasses them all.

Identifying an Existential Message[3]

With very few exceptions, an existential message always tells something about what is going on in our psyche. It has the following characteristics:

- It gives the impression that we discovered something new about us and our life, not about others;
- If it has to do with our relationships with others, then it is giving us information about the role we play in these relationships;
- It reinforces our development towards personal well-being by showing the way forward or the right decision to make;
- It gives hope;
- It brings relief;
- It comes as a surprise, precisely because it is revealing something new; or
- On the contrary, it confirms in a stronger way what we had intuited;
- It summarizes our general understanding of the dream.

An Existential Message is Not. . .

Robert Johnson (1986) identifies two possible pitfalls when trying to identify the existential message. He refers to this as the "interpretation". He suggests avoiding:

- Any interpretation that would tend to unnecessarily *inflate* your ego. If you see yourself making an interpretation where you are *peacocking* and applauding yourself for being so wonderful and superior to other mortals, then this interpretation is incorrect;
- Interpretations that take away your responsibility. It might be very tempting to take advantage of dreams to blame other persons for the events in your lives . . . These interpretations do not only lead to complacency about oneself, but they are also usually inaccurate and psychologically irrelevant.

Another pitfall would be to confuse "existential message" with "moral conscience" or "blaming". A dream is not intended to break oneself down nor to criticize oneself. It gives some *insight into* our inner world by demonstrating symbolically what is going on inside of us, somewhat like a movie.

In each method proposed, the last step is to *highlight the existential message*, which is the purpose of any dreamwork.

Nightmares

This section will be a big help for dreamers who experience recurrent nightmares. There is a lack of literature proposing specific methods for dreamwork involving nightmares, both for understanding this type of dream and for reducing their intensity and their frequency. Throughout the many years of my practice, I was able to identify seven different types of nightmares that play a variety of psychological functions. Understanding these functions might in itself be very enlightening for the dreamer. Moreover, the sequence of five steps specific to the method I developed for this particular dreamwork is unique and very efficient.

Lifelong Dream Journal Methods

I hesitated a long time before adding this chapter about *lifelong dream journals*. As the writing progressed, it became more and more important and I am now convinced that, without its inclusion, something would be missing from the book. That chapter offers an array of options for personal self-discovery, keeping in mind the passing of time. People who start writing down their dreams often do so over many decades. However, those who revisit their dream journals are relatively few. Yet, there is a lot to be learned from them: our dream journals virtually tell the story of our psychological life. This is actually the point of this chapter, which identifies 11 methods allowing us to draw wisdom from our lifelong journals. The art creations or representations of past dreams using these methods can be followed or not by dreamwork to elucidate their existential message. However, the mere presence in our environment of objects created from dreams will have a positive impact on the psyche.

I wish you a pleasant reading and a most rewarding dreamwork with creative and art therapy methods. Enjoy and have fun!

Notes

1. Free translation.
2. Free translation.
3. Both this section and the next *Identifying an existential message* and *An existential message is not. . .* were both published first in French in Hamel, J. (2017/1993). *Rêves, art-thérapie et guérison: De l'autre côté du miroir*. Montréal: Québec-Livres, and in English in Hamel, J. (2021). *Dreams, art therapy and healing: Beyond the looking glass*. London: Routledge.

1 Creative Dreamwork Methods

Introduction: What is Meant by Creative Dreamwork Methods?

This chapter presents 15 creative methods of dreamwork, assembled under six separate sections. Creativity through writing or visual art media characterizes these methods. What sets them apart from the art therapy methods presented in the next chapter is that they are simpler and faster to implement, being generally less geared towards in-depth self-exploration and self-transformation. That makes them particularly suitable to achieving relatively quick results in understanding the existential message of dreams.

Although the methods presented in this chapter might not always allow us to determine the existential message of a dream, they will at least help enhance our self-awareness. Studies have proved that merely focusing on one's dreams can have positive effects. For instance, Pesant and Zadra (2010) mention clinical results achieved in treating months-long or years-long recurring dreams, causing them to disappear after a single work session of exploration even though their meaning had not been understood.

I invite you to try all these methods at least a few times in order to familiarize yourself with each of them. That will allow you to identify your favorite ones, those that work best *for you* and are best adapted to various dream types. In addition, working consistently on your dreams will allow you to establish your own dream-deciphering style. The following sections will explain each of the 15 creative methods for dreamwork.

Jungian Amplification of Dream Images

Carl Jung – one of the first and most important analysts to explore symbols in dreams, art and imagination (Jung, 1993/1953, 1991/1958; Johnson, 1986) – developed effective methods to explore the meaning of symbols; one of these methods is *amplification.*

Working with symbols imparts them with greater effectiveness; amplifying them through representation in a drawing, painting, three-dimensional clay

DOI: 10.4324/9781003124610-2

sculpture or dream object for instance, imparts them with strong presence and impact.

Symbols are the language of the unconscious mind – a language created spontaneously in dreams, art, sandplay,[1] mental imagery or visions. Symbols play a dynamic role. When activated – through interaction with them in dreamwork, for instance – they have the power to transform us (Stein, 2009). By arousing in us a certain fascination with their images, they reveal the energy transfiguration that seeks to happen in the psyche; thus do they organize and structure our mental and emotional energy. Unconscious contents seek to become conscious through symbols.

Traditionally, Jungian symbol amplification (Johnson, 1986) allows us to broaden and deepen the scope of dream imagery; this is done by gathering information on the symbolic meaning of these images through the study of myths, fairy tales, religious traditions, archeological data, art history . . . To identify these meanings, one can consult symbol dictionaries.[2] Symbol dictionaries offer a variety of possible meanings depending on a variety of cultures; thus can they confirm the validity of intuited individual meanings. According to Johnson (1986), Jung was very surprised when he observed very ancient images and symbols in the dreams of his clients, including symbols pertaining to cultures the dreamers could not have known about.

However, we can use other tools than symbol dictionaries. We can clearly deduce the meaning of a dream by paying close attention to the imagery details. The three methods proposed here, which rely on close attention to the images and the felt sense, are based on Carl Jung's amplification method.

We call them *paying attention to dream images*. In the example below, we see that the dreamer only needed to pay specific attention to the details of his dream imagery to understand its existential message. We will then propose in this section two other methods to amplify the feelings triggered by dreams: *amplifying the felt sense in a dream* and *amplifying the felt sense upon awakening*.

Paying Attention to Dream Images

One interesting method to amplify a dream is rewriting it or telling it a second time while paying attention to the details of every visual image of the dream. If we dream of a house, what does it *visually* look like? And which house is this: is it familiar? Have we ever lived there? Do we consider it our current home even if our real home is completely different? How many rooms does it have? With what materials is it built? What colors are the walls? Are there rooms we have never actually seen? All these details can be very meaningful; thoroughly rewriting every visual detail can make the message of the dream obvious. In the same way, Gendlin (1986) suggests to recall dreams in full details, and insists on specifically recalling the *visual* images.

Application Example

Here is the dream of a man in his early sixties.

The House Close to Rough Waters

I sometimes dream that I am back in the location where my parents lived after selling the farm where I spent the first 18 years of my life. This time, the house is different. This "new" house is located at the village entrance, fronting the river. It is separated from the watercourse by the road leading to the village. This time, I dream I'm crossing the road and walking towards the shore. I walk slowly in the dirt and grass. There is no path. The slope is rather steep and I soon discover a house lying at the water's edge. The house wasn't there when my parents lived nearby. This waterfront house could be mine! I am intrigued. As I get closer to the shore, I see the front door and head that way. I smell the freshness of the air. The water carries ice chunks and as I get closer to the house, I can feel how strong the current is nearby. I enter a vestibule and examine the room to which it leads. It is a kitchen, which in turn leads to a dining room with slatted walls. The rooms are large and sport low ceilings and "modern", sixties-style dark panelling. I keep walking towards large and dark rooms. I note that the house lacks appropriate lighting. I reach a corridor that leads to another section of the house. Again, I think that it's too dark. In the middle of this corridor, there is a now-condemned door that used to open outdoors. I want to reopen the door and build a patio to "brighten" the house. I am now on the vacant lot, still close to the shore, looking at the condemned door. Again, I feel the strong current and cool air. I look at the riverbank, now wider and transformed into a large swath of earth, snow and ice with many steep crevices. I am aware of the danger of slipping and falling into the rough waters. The crevices are even more formidable and the terrain is very hilly. I am waiting for my daughter to arrive and fear for her well-being.

Dreamer's Comments

First impressions: I am as intrigued by the house – in which I could live – as by the riverbank that becomes so large that the river turns into a seashore. I make an association with the fact that I am just back from a trip to Iceland where I saw fantastic seascapes.

To apply this method, I describe the house, the riverbank and my shoreside walk with more details.

The house: it is very close to the river. It is isolated from the road by the land slope and the sound of running water. To reach the front door,

I cross a kind of wooden bridge that spans a crevice. I enter a vestibule that looks like the summer kitchen of the farmhouse where I used to live. I get closer to the center of the room. The ceiling is low, the house large. I need to bring some light into it. While looking for a solution, I notice the condemned door in the middle of the corridor. It opens outside, over-hanging the ground. I imagine a patio reminiscent of the one we recently built in my current house. But as soon as I get outside, it is the riverbank that catches my attention.

The riverbank: it changed while I was inside the house. As I emerge from the house, I find myself in a wider environment. It is a wide expanse of land and snow, with crevices that let the water in. River has turned into ocean, with churning waters filling the bottom of the crevices. Getting closer to the shoreline would be dangerous. I could slip on the snow. The crevices are now getting deeper and I see the water churning at the bottom. I can feel the danger.

I walk on the bank on hardpacked snow as if walking on ice. I'm carefully getting closer to a crevice since the ground is getting more and more slippery. I see the bottom: the water flushes in and out at a rolling boil. I look further out and see more hills and crevices. I walk away from the house and the shoreline. I feel better. The land turns wider and I find myself in something like an Icelandic landscape: a plain where one could walk forever. The further I walk, the less I hear the water. Some crevices run far inland. I like this landscape.

Existential Message

Describing the house in more detail causes me to see why I want to bring more light into it. In my new semi-retired situation, I am reconsidering my life environment, with new needs and expectations. This house represents continuity – a link to parents, roots and identity. The need to bring more light to it reflects my need to settle in a more pleasant environment for me and my current family. I want to reconfigure my house to make it more welcoming to my wife and me, and for our children when they come for short visits or to live there a little longer.

It is the outside environment that prompts me to think more deeply about the meaning of the dream and its existential message. Why did the river turn into a seaside? Do I really want to settle in a house so close to so many dangers? What dangers? How does the watery turmoil in the crevices relate to me? As I get closer to the water, I am afraid of slipping and falling into a crevice. Where does this fear of settling there come from?

I understand that the landscape surrounding the house in which I want to lay roots refers to the insecurity I feel regarding my semi-retired status.

I know that quitting full-time employment is a good decision but I want to keep "up to date"! I don't want to be retired . . . that's why I decided to tell people that I am "semi-employed" rather than "semi-retired". I want to take the time to settle in and am satisfied that the house and surroundings are appropriate for me, with an environment that is becoming larger, more turbulent, more dangerous, but alive! I like that. I want to connect with this energy and stay in the movement!

Amplifying the Felt Sense in a Dream

This method is used after the main dream-generated feeling has been identified. This can be a feeling, an emotion or a physical sensation, either felt by the dreamer (the "I") or another protagonist of the dream. It helps us dig deeper into the dream: because images are more powerful than words, drawing an emotion, a feeling or a physical sensation brings these to the fore with even more strength. This will allow us to identify, with more clarity, what they refer to in our lives. Once the corresponding situation is identified, the existential message becomes clear.

Application Example

Here is the dream of an art therapist who identified a vertigo sensation in her dream.

The Eiffel Tower

It's a beautiful day. I see a man I know, sunning himself on a chair at the foot of the Eiffel Tower. I get closer to him and see several persons relaxing in hammocks and other Tower fixtures; every level of the Tower is filled with people. I climb the Tower on foot – there is no elevator. There are suspended bridges and protective rope walls that make it impossible to fall down. The ropes look woven or entwined together. I'm at the very top and can see through a wooden suspended bridge. I look downward, from the highest vantage point I've ever experienced. I feel faint from vertigo but the view is exceptional. I feel no fear. It's impressive.

Dreamer's Comments

I apply black and white acrylic paint with my fingers, moving back and forth from inside to outside and back, trying to illustrate the feeling of vertigo I felt upon waking up. When I move inward, my hands rise as if sculpting the Eiffel Tower. The black evokes sadness wishing to leave my

Figure 1.1 **Vertigo (Reproduction).** Hand-applied black and white acrylic paint,
46 cm × 61 cm (18" × 24").

heart. As I write up my impressions, the movement evokes the beating of
a heart. The resulting image looks like fireworks.

Existential Message

The vertigo I felt in my heart and plexus is what I felt when my boyfriend
left me; it's like a roller coaster going through the heart. It's when I think
about the breakup, and realize what's happening, that it hits like vertigo.
As I write this, I realize that the breakup is associated with desertion. All
of a sudden, I see an image of vertigo and visualize myself falling in an
endless abyss reminiscent of the anxiety attacks. I felt as a teenager and
until I turned 30 – that's when I solved my problem by talking with my

mother about a desertion and death-related event that happened when I was 5 years old. I understand that the breakup revived the abandonment trauma I suffered at age five. This dream is an opportunity to live through the sadness and pain of desertion in order to heal them a bit more."

Amplifying the Felt Sense Upon Awakening

This method is particularly effective when we wake up from a dream with feelings, emotions or physical sensations without any images. These feelings are linked with waking-life experiences and can easily reveal their existential message. To facilitate dreamwork under such circumstances, we begin by asking ourselves in what body part we felt this feeling or sensation and then illustrate the feelings, sensations or emotions by drawing or painting lines, shapes and colors as experienced in that part of the body.

Application Examples

Example 1

A dreamer wakes up in the middle of the night, in tears but without any images. At first, he has no idea what generated those tears. He first seeks to identify the physical location of his sorrow and locates it near his heart, in the middle of his chest. Drawing a few lines and shapes, he illustrates the physical sensation associated with his sorrow. An image appears in his mind, a reminder of his father, dead for over ten years. As he keeps in his mind the image of his father and the difficulty he had communicating with him, he remembers a recent altercation he had with an older fellow worker. He thus understands why that altercation had such a strong impact on him: it reminded him of the difficult relationship with his father, which caused him much grief. He then becomes able to create some emotional distance with his colleague in his waking life.

Example 2

Here is another example: a nightmare with no images but with a great deal of unpleasant physical sensations upon waking up.

Dreamer's Comments

This clay sculpture (see Figure 1.2) illustrates the physical sensations I feel when I wake up from one of my recurring nightmares with no corresponding images: I wake up, curled up, stiff and drenched in sweat, with clenched teeth, stomach and muscle cramps, jaw pain, nausea and a headache, and feelings of burning, laceration, skin-puncturing needles or body-piercing spears.

I represent these nasty sensations by shaping a clay moon crescent, folded in on itself – evoking a curled-up body – and then tearing, lacerating and piercing the material. I also added some pipe cleaners – representing stomach pains – as well as black and red paint to evoke the violence and negativity of the feelings. The image evokes the darkness that takes over when apprehensions and anxieties become real

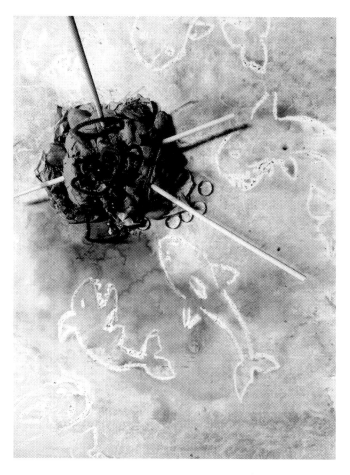

Figure 1.2 **Nightmare-generated physical sensations**. Clay sculpture and miscellaneous objects, 12½ cm diameter (5″ diameter), place on a watercolor and oil pastel painting of sharks, 46 cm × 61 cm (18″ × 24″).

and we lose control of the boat – now adrift – or when we fear being eaten by sharks.

Comments

Even though the dreamer was not aware of the nightmare contents (there are no images), assigning a three-dimensional shape to the painful physical sensations she felt at awakening had a strong impact. She established a link with a series of dreams she titled *Mother's Jaws*. By doing dreamwork on that series, she understood that her anguish set in when she considered fulfilling her mother's professional expectations for her rather than trusting her own choices. The sculpture helped her find a new resolve to trust herself and stop being thwarted by her fears and insecurities. Note that the drawing of sharks under the sculpture originates from the *Mother's Jaws* series.

Existential Message

"To you, haunting nightmare: I will not let myself be eaten alive; I will not let my fear and insecurity become a painful reality and be vulnerable."

Changing the Ending of a Dream

Once awake, several methods can be used to modify the impact of a dream ending in order to reduce its influence on one's mood and well-being. These methods teach the psyche how to change one's attitudes while dreaming, develop more harmonious and less confrontational behaviors and create more satisfying endings. The psyche learns that life can be more satisfying because, just as what we experience in waking life is reflected in dreams, what we conquer in dreams in assimilated in waking life. Three methods can be used to change the impact of dream endings: *positive art, four-steps dream* and *gift giving.*

Positive Art

Positive art is a very simple, fast and effective method of making important attitudinal changes in waking life, by simply drawing a different ending to a dream – a more positive and calming one. Understanding the language of imagery, the psyche will begin creating new neuronal circuits, replacing negative programming with other ways of perceiving life. According to Jobin (2021, 2020, 2017), positive art is well suited to that purpose, particularly for anxiety-filled dreams. You first draw, without changing anything, what has been seen in the dream, and then do a second drawing about what you wish to change.

Doing the first drawing with the disturbing image gives a sense of what kind of a new image and new outlook on life you want to create.

Application Example

After an anxiety-filled dream,[3] a young woman decided to use this method to work on her dream (see Figure 1.3):

A Bridge to the Void

I dream of a great void with a very sharp and eroded rock in its middle; over it there is a great darkness, a dense fog, a gloomy atmosphere. To get to the rock, there is a wood plank bridge with no supporting pillars; the bridge just hangs in the void. The planks are broken, ridden with holes, and the whole assembly seems rickety. To reach the rock, I have to walk on the bridge but I'm afraid to continue walking. After a few steps, I turn back towards the solid ground. I'm holding on to the netted edge. I can't decide whether I want to continue on or go back. I wake up in the morning feeling anguish.

Figure 1.3 **The suspension bridge**. Collage of a watercolor image, 21 cm × 27½ cm (8½" × 11").

Comments

The dreamer decides to create a collage, selecting an image that is different from the derelict bridge of her dream. She likes her chosen image because it shows a solid suspension bridge and more importantly, a bright destination. This image gives her hope that her life can become more positive, that she can have a happy future. Looking often at the positive image or collage fosters positive emotions, day by day.

One year later, I spoke with the young woman about her experience. She had no recollection of her nightmare; she only remembered this positive image!

Four-Steps Dream

Kaplan-Williams (1987) proposes the "Four Quadrants" dream method, whereby you draw the dream in three acts and then create a fourth drawing depicting a resolution of the dream drama. You can even draw what you imagine happened *before* the dream; what is important is to end with a fourth scene that shows a satisfying conclusion to the dream. This is a simple and very effective method for initiating inner change. You can place the scenes in a large circle – like a four-section mandala[4] – or on four separate sheets. The apparent simplicity of this method can be deceiving; in fact, it triggers an immediate inner change by suggesting a satisfying ending to the dream. Here is the anxiety-filled dream of France Raymond d'Aragon, a well-known artist in Montréal, Québec, Canada.

Application Example

Crossing the Red Bridge

I dream I'm on a road; there is an emergency. It's nighttime. Right across from my neighbor's house and on the other side of the road, there is a bridge. I'm with my partner and we must cross that red bridge but there is some kind of a storm; the river is overflowing its banks and submerging the bridge. The bridge is unsafe, shaken by the vicious waves.

I start running and manage to cross the bridge; once on the other side, I turn around and see that an older woman has also managed to cross, right behind me. My partner is on his way; he reaches me and wants to take me in his arms and to my surprise, his face is that of another man's – an unknown bearded man.

Dreamer's Comments

My current life context is as follows: I feel divided and scattered and am trying to restore my unity. This is a time of questioning about the rest of my life. I am involved in many different activities: I am a visual artist – a painter – and bear my maternal grandmother's name: D'Aragon. I am a counselling therapist and conduct art and creativity workshops. I am wondering if I should go back to school to become an art therapist.

At 57, I don't know how I want to live this new life stage, including life as a couple. My children are now grown up and on their own; my daughter lives in Berlin and my son has his own place.

The day before, I consulted a French energy therapist; we spoke about my grandmother's energy, about autoimmune disease, about not knowing if I can trust my own body, and about my life as a solitary little girl who had to create her own bubble to survive. I am fully aware of the fear and anger that have been mine since early childhood – so far removed and yet so near.

Comments

The dreamer decides to explore her dream using the four-steps dream method. For her first image, she draws what happens at the beginning of the dream (see Figure 1.4): a woman and a man standing near the starting point of the red-pink bridge. The woman's dress is almost the same color as the color of the bridge and the man wears dark blue clothes. The bridge is red but veiled by the water splashing over it. It is supported by three brown beams. As she looks at the drawing, the feelings and emotions that come to her mind are rigidity, apprehension, fear of the unknown, concern and an urgent need to cross the bridge.

She then draws the second scene of her dream: the flooded red bridge (see Figure 1.5), with two legs, very dynamic blue and white lines curving above and below the bridge. On the right side of the image, she notices a smooth and very bright yellow surface. She also sees that the space is clearer on the left side, where there is something like a ghost town in the distance. As she looks at this drawing, the feelings and emotions that come to her mind are agitation, invasion, confusion, an impression of dirtiness and what she perceives as the bridge's rigidity.

The third image (see Figure 1.6) shows what happens in the middle of the dream: the woman in red-pink clothing, followed by the woman in white in the middle and the man in the rear. In this image, she makes special note of the red-pink rectangle representing the bridge and the three figures surrounded by blue threads – reminiscent of barbed wire or electric wires. They are almost trapped by the water and blue wires. There is also a very present yellow section and a clearing in the upper left corner. As she looks at this drawing, she feels trapped, stuck, stifled

Figures 1.4 and 1.5 ***Crossing the red bridge 1 and 2.*** Dry pastel, 46 cm × 61 cm
(18″ × 24″).

and in danger; the feelings and emotions that come to her mind are fear, uncertainty, disgust, anger, tiredness and exhaustion.

For the fourth and last image (see Figure 1.7), the dreamer reflects on what she would change in her dream: *I would remove all those electrical wires and all the water submerging the bridge. I would put the water back where it belongs – the bridge would set its limits! I would remove all the confusion.*

Figures 1.6 and 1.7 **Crossing the red bridge, 3 and 4**. Dry pastel, 46 cm × 61 cm (18″ × 24″).

Her resolution image – the one she imagines as a satisfying solution to the dream – becomes: *A bright orange path overhanging a calmer, more civilized, milder watercourse. The couple walks together and a ghost-like, white-robed, somewhat surreal woman precedes them, appearing to float in the air. She is strangely suspended between earth and sky. The bridge is supported by brown beams and lined with pink posts on either side for protection. Everything is in its place; the water stays below the bridge and the path is clear. I notice that I find the ghostly woman puzzling and disturbing. I see that the bridge is a different color; for me, orange is the color of the sexuality and creativity chakra.*

Existential Message

Drawing a dream-resolution image makes it easier to apprehend the existential message of the dream. Here is what the dreamer writes: *What I see in the image is a couple walking "together"; it moves me very deeply. Everything is back in place; there is less danger; I can be myself; I'm no longer in danger, nor overwhelmed by emotions. At last, I can breathe.*

By itself, the dream does not provide an answer to the dreamer's questioning of her own life plans; the dream doesn't tell her if a Master of Arts in Art Therapy is a pertinent choice for her. However, the dream-resolution image delivers a very important message: *"You can do what you want; you have sorted out your inner turmoil and are free to go wherever you see fit."* That message is thereafter confirmed through her Jungian dialogue[5] with the "White Lady".

Jungian dialogue[6] with the White Lady
Who are you? What are you doing here?
White Lady: I am you guardian angel, a part of you that exists since you were born, and I am watching over you. I love you and I care about you.
Tell me what's happening in the image.
White Lady: I am ready to leave because you don't need me anymore. From now on you will be able to live and enjoy your earthly life. It is time for you to trust yourself and to continue with your life. It is time for you to be as bold as your projects. It is time to stop being afraid, to trust yourself and to trust life. The path ahead is radiant. Let life support you.

Gift Giving

Several authors, among them Garfield (1999) and Kaplan-Williams (1987), have introduced us to the Senoï tribe in their books; this is a people whose dreams have a great influence on their waking lives. The Senoï observe three major rules *while* dreaming: always fight and overcome dangers (as when meeting an enemy in a dream); always seek pleasure, whether sexual or other; and always achieve a positive outcome. To this end, they learn to always ask for a gift or find treasure while dreaming (Garfield, 1999). In the morning, they describe their dreams to one another and decide what needs to be done during the day to use the collective wisdom revealed by the dreams. One of the instructions they observe is to offer to members of the community – or themselves – the gifts they have seen in their dreams; this includes giving presents to tribe members to offset any negative behavior they might have had towards them in a dream. A tribe member who hurts someone in a dream can atone for the "deed" by making a present to give to the aggrieved party, or make sure to be friendly with him/her during the day.

If you received a gift in a dream or found or observed a treasure or work of art, it would be a good idea to reproduce it for yourself. Conversely, if you physically or verbally abused or hurt someone in a dream, you probably hurt a part of yourself as a result. In such a case, it might be a good idea to make a "present", a painting, an object, a treasure, to repair that part of you and check what impact that action has on you. That part of you will likely respond favorably to the action, which will increase your inner well-being. You can also choose to perform a simple symbolic mending ritual.

Here is an example of someone receiving something that can surely be considered a "treasure":

Application Example

The Wedding Ring

A man and a woman give me a small round golden box. They entrust it to me, asking me to take good care of it. I lift the lid, see a plastic film under which is a wedding ring. I remove the film, pick up the ring to examine it, and put it back in the box. There is a mark showing where the ring should be placed. The man and the woman aren't there anymore (see Figure 1.8).

Dreamer's Comments

After making the box and ring, I was simultaneously sad and happy. Happy because I felt that this had something to do with healing, with a path I had just discovered. This spoke of an alliance with myself, of a new balance between my feminine and masculine aspects. I felt joyful. But sad also because I felt I should have found that path long ago and was afraid I might not be capable of doing so. While looking at the

Figure 1.8 ***The treasure box and the ring.*** Cardboard, plastic film, golden silk paper, 11 cm (4¾″) diameter.

finished box, I suffered from all kinds of physical ailments – stomach ache, nausea, painful sternum . . . I just accepted the pains and they finally went away.

As I slipped the ring on my finger, a new pleasant feeling settled in the core of my body, what felt like some kind of contact with my center, in the middle of my body.

Spontaneous Reactions

Two methods allow to explore dreams through spontaneous reactions: *spontaneous writing* and *developed scribbling*. Whether written or drawn, spontaneous reactions carry much information on what is happening in the psyche.

Spontaneous Writing

Anne-Marie Jobin (2017/2013) taught me this method. She suggests writing three pages spontaneously to explore a specific theme: you quickly write down whatever goes through your head, without much thinking, and then extract the existential message, somewhat like Julia Cameron's three morning pages (2010). Like other creative methods, spontaneous writing can easily reveal the existential message of a dream.

One variant involves writing with your non-dominant hand, from which often emerges a different kind of inner voice, more unconscious and primitive.

Application Example

The Helicopter

My husband says to me: "Do you want to come for a helicopter ride above the city? You've never been in a helicopter." He is the one piloting the helicopter.

Here is an example of spontaneous writing inspired by this dream. I wrote this at the end of a convention on dreams. As you will see, I spontaneously write down whatever pops into my head:

What does this dream mean? I have no idea! I can find no immediate association and it seems far removed from my reality! I think of my brother who pilots amphibious planes but I don't think he took helicopter-flying lessons . . . the truth is that I've never gone on a helicopter ride and I've never had the opportunity or inclination to do so.

An association comes to mind with my partner, who is driving me: we are leaving today to go back home and the trip will take a few days since the convention on dreams just ended in Virginia Beach.[7] I'll admit that dreamwork is a little like flying over reality, but this is a familiar activity, something I do regularly, not really foreign to my reality.

And the city? It looks like a big city. What this suggests to me is: flying above, looking from on high, looking from afar, looking at the big picture, moving away from down to earth attitudes . . . those words speak to me more. I feel that this convention is feeding and growing my passion for dreams.

Working on dreams takes me away from daily life, from down to earth experiences, and something in me likes that very much. It gives me a wider perspective than my daily routine. And riding a helicopter is not like riding a plane: the helicopter stays closer to the reality down below than a plane flying at 30,000 feet.

Riding a helicopter gives you enough distance to understand a city's urban plan, the structure of the neighborhoods that form the city; that would give me a general view of the downtown core, the outskirts, the rivers that cut across it, the roads that crisscross it . . . and it would be high enough to get away from the noise and bustle of life on the ground. No other association comes to mind for the moment.

Getting away just enough from everyday concerns reminds me of my dreamwork, which entails taking time for myself, time for my inner life, time for taking a step back from everyday events, time for acquiring a larger sense of what is happening in my psyche.

Since I don't know what more to write, I'll go back to the images of my dream. Among other things, I'm curious about my husband flying the helicopter. What is the meaning of his invitation to join him in the helicopter for a ride above the city? The city can't be Virginia Beach because in my dream, the image I get is of a much larger American city, perhaps Minneapolis . . . I just had a thought: is it significant that he is inviting me to ride with him because he already is in the helicopter? He's handling the controls and flying slightly above me when he launches the invitation. At least that's the image that comes to mind when I think about the dream . . . that's it, I think I understand!

Of the notions above, two speak to me more and put me on the right track to find the existential message of the dream: one, that my partner is already in the helicopter when he invites me to join; and two, the notion of looking at the big picture, of taking a step back, of moving away from the city's brouhaha. These two notions make me realize that I'm still working full time and that part of me is yearning for being calmer and more distanced from the turbulent aspects of my work. It is really when I realize that my partner is already flying the helicopter that insight hits me and that the meaning of the dream emerges more clearly. The existential message is that like many others, I am also yearning for early retirement, seeking to move away from my frenetic work schedule, eager to adopt a different work rhythm.

Comments

It is attention to the visual details that caused the dreamer to understand the existential message of her dream; and it is the brisk, spontaneous writing process that brought about this level of attention, effortlessly. Spontaneous writing is a simple method of finding, without too much effort, the existential message of dreams.

Developed Scribbling

Developed scribbling is widely used in art therapy. I learned the technique in the 1980s from my art therapy teachers Lillian Rhinehart and Paula Engelhorn, who taught at the Eagle Rock Art Therapy Institute, in Santa Rosa, California.

As a first step, you draw a series of lines in all directions with a black pencil, creating a meaningless doodle.

At this stage, it is important to refrain from using colored pencils; their use could well induce the image to acquire a certain direction. It is also important to resist the temptation to "make nice" and to avoid filling the paper sheet too much or too little. Using the largest sheet possible – ideally 46 × 61 cm (18″ × 24″) – will be helpful. When the sheet has been covered with random lines, you gaze at it until you detect a figurative image on either side of the paper. You will generally find several such images; select the one that attracts or intrigues you the most.

You then develop the chosen image. This is done by emphasizing the lines that compose the image and adding more lines to make it even more obvious. The next step is to color the drawing, using only the lines that work best for you; there is no need to use all the doodle lines. The image can be developed on another sheet or within the original doodle itself. When the image is fully developed, you ponder what the image could tell you about your dream: if it might be a comment on the existential message of the dream, what might the comment be?

At the end of Chapter 3, you will find an example of a doodle that was drawn to explore the nightmare entitled *The Outhouse in the Fields* (See Figure 3.3). The doodle alone was enough to reveal an essential part of the information that was needed to understand the message of the nightmare.

Metaphor and Contra-Metaphor

What characterizes the metaphor/contra-metaphor method is that it uses positive or negative exaggeration of the dream contents to bring to light the message of the dream. Two methods can be used to that effect: *using analogy* (positive exaggeration of the dream content) and *drawing or painting the dream opposite* (negative exaggeration of the dream content).

Metaphor: Using Analogy

This method requires revisiting the dream with the assumption that everything that happens in it is an exact analogy to what happens in your life. For certain dreams, that is enough for the message to instantly become evident. It is possible to foster awareness by rewriting the dream, adding the following words after each sentence: *and that's the story of my life* or *and that's what's going on in my life at the moment*. When I use this method in a therapeutic context, I just repeat the dream for my client, amplifying the analogies. Often the message immediately becomes clear.

Application Example

The Abandoned Factory

I'm going down to the lower levels of a factory with a team of men. I'm not sure what we're going to do there. I keep going down. A picture then comes to my mind, of a page of my personal diary on which I'm painting something. I see an assembly of criss-crossing, meaningless yellow and red doodles. I keep going down and see another page on which I'm drawing another doodle. Everything in the factory is grey and empty.

Everything in these spaces is gloomy. I have a feeling that we should leave this place urgently.

Dreamer's Comments

I rewrite the dream and in certain places, I add: "and that's what's going on in my life at the moment":

I'm going down into gray and gloomy spaces where everything is empty, and that's what's going on in my life at the moment. The only place where there is color is in my personal diary and that's what's going on in my life at the moment. I urgently need to leave this gray space and that's what's going on in my life at the moment.

Existential Message

The message I receive is that because my work has become very time-consuming and rather "gray", I feel that I have neglected my inner life lately, failing to write in my diary and paint. I urgently need to resume doing that.

Contra-Metaphor: Drawing or Painting the Dream Opposite

As you will see in this example, a good method of identifying an existential message is to go against part of the dream. The contrast helps bring the message of the dream to awareness.

Application Example

A dreamer holidaying in a warm country has had nightmares two nights in a row, waking up in the morning in a somewhat similar state of panic. As she opens her door one evening during the same period, she sees some kind of big round spider watching her in the dark through two small white eyes; wrapped around it is what looks like hairs or ribbons. Later on, she will wonder if that was real since it was so surprising. For some mysterious reason, that spider seems to be linked to both nightmares. Here are her two anxiety-filled dreams.

First Dream: Anguish in the Sea

I'm outdoors in a tropical place. I'm waiting for my boss to arrive. A female friend takes the place behind the wheel of a van in which we're waiting for the boss. She backs up to position the van so that it is ready to leave. She asks me what direction to take. I answer that I don't know.

Right in front of me is the ocean. I swim in it and all of a sudden, my feet lose contact with the bottom. A wave is dragging me offshore. I think I'm going to drown and tell myself: "No, stop, don't panic". I start swimming. I try telling my faraway friend that I can't come back. I tell myself: "No, stop, you have to conserve your energy". I see myself in the water as if I were swimming underwater. I know I can't come back and that I'm going to drown.

I wake up, my heart beating hard. I'm anguished, scared and short of breath. I shiver, my skin is clammy and my blood vessels are throbbing. I tell myself: "Don't panic".

Second Dream: Earthquake at the Convention

A colleague of mine, friend of the boss, has organized a convention. She is the main organizer. Since I'll be on leave for a while, I'm not part of the organizing team. Few people show up. After the first day, the convention is so boring that many people are leaving.

I leave. As I'm walking down the convention hotel staircase, the ground starts shaking. Pieces of the hotel are falling down. This is an earthquake. I find myself in a cave. Everything's shaking around me. I hear rocks falling. I shut my eyes, I'm scared and my heart is beating hard. I tell myself: "This must be what dying means". I wake up almost in the same condition as the previous day but it is less intense.

Dreamer's Comments

I have always had such intense emotions that I feel my heart is too small. My heart is like the black spider; it holds so many very intense emotions that I fear I won't be able to contain them: shame, sadness, jealousy, envy, anger, resentment, fear of anguish, anxiety. It is all about the fear of dying . . . fear of dying alone and abandoned, of remaining alone, of dying alone without anybody noticing. . .

Comments: In fact, as far back as she can remember, she has always had the feeling that nobody acknowledged her existence; her parents, notably her father, never took notice of her distress, anguish and need to be reassured.

The dreamer decides to use the *contra-metaphor* method, by *painting the opposite of her dream*. Since seeing the spider seem to be linked to her dreams, she will paint the opposite of the black spider: it will exude all kinds of colors that for her, represent playing the piano, singing, dancing . . . standing up, she imagines and mimics playing the piano in front of others, something she's always unable to do. While her hands play the piano on the paper sheet, she applies yellow paint. She adds some green because singing seems to be of that color. She first sings some soul music, she then becomes a soprano and sings

Figure 1.9 ***Colors coming out of the black spider.*** Finger paint, 46 cm × 61 cm (18″ × 24″).

some light opera music, then a lullaby, and she finishes up with some singing exercises. She would like to dance, for which she has no need of a human escort. She can dance either alone or with someone else because dancing is a passion; she applies some red paint on the paper sheet, her fingers gracefully sliding, gently dancing like a bird's flight (see Figure 1.9).

Thanks to this exploration, she understands that her lifeforce has been unavailable to her until now. She has a choice to make: she can either lock her feelings up in her heart and continue to fear death, or express herself, let it be, and make herself present in the eyes of others. She discovers that expression is life. The color explosion was hidden in her heart, as in the black spider image. The most important existential message of the dream is that she needs to exist in her own eyes, meaning that she can relax and allow herself to live and express herself.

A few weeks later, I get a note from this person, telling me that letting the colors come out on the paper sheet – while mimicking herself playing the piano, singing, dancing the bird's flight – has had an important grounding effect. Moving her body *has started life flowing inside her*. That moment has triggered a transformation she feels daily, she tells me.

Haïkus

Traditionally, Haïkus are Japanese poems that comprise three lines of five, seven and five syllables respectively. I have discovered three ways to use Haïkus for dreamwork: *written Haïku, visual Haïku* and *triptych*.

Written Haïku

Several authors mention Haïkus, including Jobin (2015) and Mellick (2001) who recognize their value for working with dreams of which few images remain. Generally, Haïkus begin with a season or physical location in the first line, followed by an action in the second line and a surprising or unexpected element in the third. When applied to a dream, the assembly can effectively summarize the emotional issue of the dream. To maximize its impact, it is important that the Haïku be brief and composed of vivid images.

Psychologist, art therapy professor and art therapist Sophie Boudrias uses Haïkus when she wakes up, as a way to better remember her dream before she can write it down later in the day. In the first line, she writes down the triggering element; in the second, the action or development; and in the third, the outcome or ending of the dream. Composing Haïkus also helps her quickly understand and memorize the existential message of a dream. Moreover, she uses Haïkus as incubation instruments to generate specific dream types or ask for specific answers to everyday problems.

Application Example

A Yellowing Plant

I'm on an Indian reservation. I'm walking with a woman from the front to the side of the house where there is a cedar shingle wall, gray with age. There is a long bench alongside the wall, spanning its whole length. On the bench, there are potted plants. I must pick a pot. I choose one with a plant that is starting to yellow. I don't know if it will live or die. I'm disappointed and surprised at my choice.

Haïku

An Indian reservation
I choose a flower pot
Will the plant live or die?

You will notice that the dreamer does not necessarily abide by the traditionally prescribed number of syllables. It doesn't matter because what is important with this method is to use it to get a grasp of the dream, by using the strongest images possible. In the example above, the Haïku poses an important existential question: will this part of herself live or die? To further her exploration, the dreamer uses the method below.

Visual Haïku

Visually representing the most striking image of your Haïku by means of drawing, painting or collage is likely to make the message of the dream even more obvious. Sometimes, visual representation is essential to identify the existential message of the dream.

Application Example

Following her previous dream and Haïku, the dreamer decides to illustrate the flower even if she feels somewhat anxious about her choice in the dream. After it has been drawn, I pull away the paper sheet so that she can view the flower from a distance (see Figure 1.10). Seized with emotion, she says to me: "*It's not dead! It's not yellowing! Yellow is her natural color!*" When she looks at the drawing, she feels exactly what she felt when she slipped the ring on her finger (see the Application Example in Gift Giving, and Figure 1.8). The drawing connects her with the sensation she has been feeling in the core of her body since she wore the ring on her finger.

Comments

The dreamer understands that this dream evokes her self-doubt and that the path she mentioned while working on the ring (see Figure 1.8) involves self-confidence, trusting her own feelings, keeping in contact with what she feels in her body, and self-centering in order not to lose sight of herself. *And to achieve this*, she says, *I must do something for myself, spend time with myself, just to keep centered.* She names the flower "Being in centration".

Existential Message

The dream reminds me that I should take the time to nourish my core by keeping contact with the feelings in the center of my body and taking time to be alone, just to keep centered.

Triptych

To follow up on a Haïku, you can also paint three Haïku scenes or you can create a triptych that will depict the impactful history of the poem in three steps.

Être dans la centration
c'est ma voie

Figure 1.10 ***Being centered.*** Wooden coloring pencils, about 15 cm (6″) diameter.

The following example uses the same subject three times, which makes it useful for clarifying the existential message.

Application Example

The "Fabergé" Egg

I dream that I see my friend Johanne sitting at a table on top of which there is an egg. She wants to create a work of art and I hear the words: "It will be a Fabergé egg". She gets ready to decorate the egg.

Haïku

> *An egg*
> *A work of art*
> *A Fabergé Egg*

Dreamer's Comments

Following this dream, I decorated three Styrofoam eggs (See Figure 1.11). While decorating them, I understood that something new was unfolding

Figure 1.11 ***"Fabergé" eggs.*** Styrofoam, gel pens, sparkles and acrylic paint; each egg measures 8 cm × 2 cm (3¼″ × 4¾″).

in me. I was finalizing my doctorate – the subject of which was artistic creation – and my artist identity was emerging. The thrice-repeated message through the creation of these mandala eggs slowly became evident to me.

Programming a Dream Through Visual Art

This method affords two possible choices: you can program a dream that you wish to have, meaning that you can use the image to "incubate a dream". You can also program a change you wish for in a recurring dream by visually illustrating that change. This is an important method to use when dealing with recurring dreams, to avoid difficult situations from consistently repeating themselves in your dreams.

Incubating a Dream Through Visual Art

Visually illustrating what you wish to achieve through incubation is similar to positive visualization techniques. Although having a clear and precise intention regarding the dream you want to achieve benefits incubation, having an image that suggests it is even more effective. For example, if you wish to fly like a bird, make sure to draw, paint or find an image of a flying bird or person. If you dream of securing a book-writing contract in a dream, draw a book with your author's name on the cover . . . try this and you will see how well the power of image works. Over the years, I have had countless opportunities to witness the power and effectiveness of collages and images as visualization instruments.

Application Example

A man, who has been traveling extensively through the deserts of Arizona and California wishes to revisit those places in his dreams. He likes and appreciates the feeling of vastness, the sense of eternity and deep peacefulness he experiences when he travels and camps there several weeks at a time. He would like to relive these feelings in his dreams, as a means to living his spirituality. He composes a collage made up of the photographs that bring back the strongest memories he has of these moments (see Figure 1.12).

Figure 1.12 Collage of travel photographs in western USA (This portion should be in black and in italics). Photos on paper, 46 × 61 cm (18″ × 24″).

Recurring Dream Changing

Let yourself draw, paint or represent the changes you wish to achieve in recurring dreams. For example, if you often lose your wallet or your way and cannot find any help to remedy the situation, you can represent your recovered wallet or a signposted road or find a picture of a helping person. You will obtain even better results if you leave this image, drawing, painting or collage in your immediate vicinity so that you can look at it regularly.

Application Example

The Toilet

When the dream begins, I am entering a large room that seems to be located in a secondary school. A social event is taking place – a reception, happy hour or something of that nature. My life partner, whom I can't see, is on my right. There are people around but I can't really see them either. Facing me and to the left, I see a swimming pool and further away, large bay windows.

I move towards the other side of the pool, walking through the water. I notice that my shoes and pant bottoms are in the water but I don't care.

On the other side, somebody emerges from behind a green – almost khaki – curtain. That's where the toilet is located and that's where I'm going because I have to pee. So I get behind this curtain, which hangs from a pole supported by two posts. As I pull the curtain back in place, I notice that it's not as opaque as I had thought when I was on its other side, from where I couldn't see through it. Now, depending on the viewing angle, I notice that I can see through it. Which means that people can partially see me.

On the floor is a large transparent plastic bag containing several pieces of white cotton underwear, similar to what boys used to wear when I was a little girl. Some of them have yellow urine spots, others not. I tell myself that this is where people come to urinate and that I'm going to take a clean pantie.

I am squatting above these pieces of underwear, bare-assed, and see that this toilet is wide open on both sides. On my left, at a certain distance, I see a group of youths. I am thinking that they can see me and notice that one of the boys is looking at me. I am embarrassed, but then I tell myself that it's too bad that he will see my bum and I'm going to pee because I have to! Its only buttocks, after all. And I wake up.

Comments: The theme of this dream is pretty frequent, when people feel exposed and vulnerable in some social situation. For her, it is a recurring dream, although in itself it is not always the same one: usually,

*Figure 1.13 **The toilet**.* Oil pastels, 46 × 61 cm (18″ × 24″).

because of a space that lacks proper intimacy to urinate or defecate, she won't be able to enjoy the social event she is attending in her dream.

The dreamer draws a different ending to this dream: the toilet walls are solid and there is a clean toilet bowl (See Figure 1.13). She will be safe to urinate and will then be able to enjoy the social event in which people are dancing, celebrating and having fun. By creating a stark contrast with the frustrating situation in the dream, the dreamer was able to understand the message of the dream.

Dreamer's Comments on the Existential Message of the Dream

I need to set up a space that corresponds to my nature, in order to nurture a part of me that needs to be developed. A space where this part of me will be able to express itself without being in a vulnerable state. A place where that part can be "updated", where I'll be able to settle down completely – or perhaps loosen up – with more poise and self-confidence.

Conclusion

In conclusion, what you need to do now is try these creative methods! Use them regularly and experiment with several of them. That's how you will be able to identify those that work best for you and those with which you have the most affinities. Observe their impact on your personal transformation: you most probably will gain inner peace and suffer less turmoil, agitation, anxiety or unpleasant emotions.

Notes

1. Sandplay is a psychotherapeutic method whereby the client is invited to create an imaginary scene by placing a variety of miniature figurines in a sand-filled box. For more details, see Chapter 2.
2. However, I do not recommend the use of dream dictionaries, which are all very different from one another and assign predetermined meanings to dream imagery – something to be avoided.
3. This dream – but not this image – was first mentioned in Hamel, J. (2017/1993). *Rêves, art-thérapie et guérison*. Montréal: Québec-Livres, and in Hamel, J. (2021). *Dreams, art therapy and healing: Beyond the looking glass*. New York: Routledge.
4. *Mandala* is a Sanscrit word meaning 'circle'. Mandalas are usually separated into four parts or multiples of four. They are universal, being found in all religions or thought systems – Christian, Buddhist, etc. Mandalas begin appearing in children's drawings at age 3 or 4 (Kellog, 2016).
5. See Chapter 2.
6. See Chapter 2.
7. This was the 32nd Convention of the *International Association for the Study of Dreams* (IASD), in 2015.

2 Art Therapy Dreamwork Methods

Introduction

Nine art therapy dreamwork methods are introduced in this chapter: *dream re-entry through images, collage, mask making, clay sculpture, storytelling, sand-play, embodying the dream*, as well as *color exploration* and finally, *healing rituals*. These methods all use a wider range of means and art media beyond simply drawing, painting and sculpting.[1] They complement and add a wide variety to the basic methods I use for art therapy dreamwork.

These methods are called *art therapeutic* because art psychotherapists use them in their practice and all of these methods make use of plastic art media typical of art therapy. They are presented here as a means to self-explore one's dreaming life, with the understanding that one will seek professional help if needed, in the event that too much inner discomfort is caused by that type of work. One should keep in mind that any psychological work that was opened by means of images has to be closed off by means of images as well, hence the need to choose an art psychotherapist to complete deep inner work using images.

Art therapy is a preferred approach not only for elucidating the dream's message, but also for working on one's self-transformation and for developing one's inner consciousness. The methods outlined here thus allow for going beyond identifying the dream's existential message; indeed, they provide the opportunity to do effective self-work. By interacting with the psyche's images, understanding them and transforming them using the various methods suggested in this chapter, the very essence of our inner world, its psychic content, can be transformed for the better.

In many instances, the existential message of a dream is immediately made obvious through art creation, simply because we are contemplating images in great detail. In some cases, a deep sense of peace and fulfillment arises from breathing life into an inner reality on paper, or through a three-dimensional representation (clay, mask making, physical object, etc.). Carl Jung (1993) stated that giving shape to an image from the unconscious mind indeed has therapeutic effects in itself. Art actually allows our inner experience to be expressed in a material reality; the image is now something outside of ourselves and we are influenced by its concrete presence.

DOI: 10.4324/9781003124610-3

Three Common Steps for the Art Therapy Dreamwork Methods[2]

The same three steps apply to each of the nine methods, possibly with slight differences depending on the characteristics of the selected art medium. Initially, we will remind you what these three steps are, in general terms, then the suggested procedures will be detailed more specifically for each of the different art therapy dreamwork methods.

Step #1: Exploring the primordial image of a dream with art media
Step #2: Finding meaning in the art experience (three ways)
Step #3: Identifying the existential message

Step #1: Exploring the Primordial Image of a Dream with Art Media

There is no need to know how to paint, draw or have experience with art media to benefit from the full impact of this step. The mere act of visually translating into colors, lines and shapes the primordial image or impression of a dream as a whole promotes the awareness of aspects that otherwise would have remained unnoticed. This work also brings out the emotional reaction, the very one we need to understand the meaning of a dream.

The importance of the evocative power of images was explained previously. Giving images a physical reality by means of drawing, painting or other media allows for revealing their full impact. These explorations through art provide access to a deep experience. At Step #2, writing your thoughts following this exploration will help you go further into understanding the dream's existential message.

Step #2: Finding Meaning in the Art Experience (Three Ways)

Now that an art production was created, it is useful to put words on it to easily elucidate the meaning of your dream. In the next pages, I suggest three written exercises to put our inner experience from Step #1 into words.

Spontaneous Reactions and Associations to Artwork

Very often, our reactions to artwork production and all that we went through while creating offer all the information needed to elucidate a dream's existential message. The mere act of reproducing a dream's image with art materials causes a wide range of reactions. It also causes spontaneous associations with the image that appear before our eyes. All these reactions are not pulled out of thin air; they are loaded with unexpected clues about the meaning of the dream. That is why, at this stage, any spontaneous reaction should be noted so that you can draw the appropriate conclusions thereafter. What is worth noting in particular? Anything that prompted a response during artwork creation may have meaning; the following is a non-exhaustive list.

You may take note of your reactions to:

- A part of the plastic artwork production you dislike; or
- On the contrary, a part you particularly like;
- Different types of lines and shapes;
- The colors you used and how they impact you;
- The images that appeared, even if they are different from what the dream inspired;
- The overall impression that is conveyed; for example, a figure that is staged in a large white space might give rise to some fears in you, or on the contrary bring a sense of comfort, or a creepy mask may feel frightening, etc.;
- The medium that was used (gouache, pastels, felt pens, finger paint, watercolors, modeling clay, fabrics or other materials) and any sensation caused by these mediums, such as satisfaction, frustration, etc.;
- Any other reaction you might have had during the creative process.

The dream's existential message may well arise from these brief notes.

Identification to Dream Images

The second approach is the Gestalt method of identifying with dream images (Hamel, 1997; Rhyne, 1984).[3] The following written tool, as well as the next one, were developed in collaboration with my colleague, psychologist and art therapist Lorraine Dumont. After producing an image from the dream, use writing to identify to the image, as follows:

- Describe the image as well as the impression that emerges from it, as precisely as possible, using qualifiers, as if you were trying to explain it to someone who does not see it. It's not a matter of rewriting the whole dream, but of distancing yourself from it to describe only the image or object that is now in front of you.
- Read your writings again, assuming for a moment it accurately describes a current aspect of yourself or your life. Take note of any reaction to this experience.
- Complete the following sentences, choosing from among these:

    o   Thanks to you, I am becoming aware that I am. . .
    o   I now feel. . .
    o   I am deciding that. . .

Dialogue with Dream Images

The Jungian dialogue is another way of working on dream images after artwork reproduction. This is a particularly appropriate method when the meaning of a dream remains elusive, or when a dream carries archetypal figures, in other words very impressive figures either positive or negative, since it makes it possible to avoid identifying with it directly, which may often cause discomfort.

It's about asking questions, listening to the answers that come up and then writing them down. The greatest challenge is to avoid fabricating an answer, and to make sure to listen to the answers emerging from the core of your being. When an answer comes as a surprise to you, it is a sign that you are on the right track.

The following questions may serve as a guide:

- Who are you?
- Why is it that you look like that?
- What does your life look like?
- What are you doing in my dream?
- Do you embody an aspect of myself?
- Do you have any message for me?
- Any other question that sparks a curiosity in you.

This is an "active dialogue", since we need to be involved in the sharing. We do this by communicating what we agree with, our refusals, our objections and maybe even our fearful reactions to dream characters or images. You might want to write a few pages for each dialogue.

Step #3: Identifying the Existential Message

Once you have reproduced or created a dream's image and noted what you experienced, all you have to do is to word the dream's existential message in a short sentence. Although it often contains wisdom applicable to human life as a whole, an existential message is useful to the extent that it relates to a specific situation in your current life. At this point, your graphic creation and writings should have allowed you to see how the events or concerns in your waking life relate to the dream's symbols.

Example for these Three Steps

The following dream will serve to illustrate the three steps.

Step #1: Drawing or Painting A Dream Figure

The simplest way to apply the first step, which is about exploring the primordial image of a dream using an art medium, obviously is to draw or paint one of the dream's scenes. This dream is from a woman in her fifties who is going through post-traumatic stress disorder (PTSD) after experiencing sexual assault. The old adage about a picture being worth a thousand words is quite appropriate in this instance. Indeed, drawing or painting a figure from a dream (character or object) allows details from the imagery to arise that might not necessarily have been noticed when telling the dream story. Unexpected details provide significant clues to understand the existential message.

The Rusty Bicycle

I see a red rusty bicycle in my dream.

*Figure 2.1 **The rusty bicycle**. Oil pastels, 46 × 61 cm (18″ × 24″).*

Step #2: Putting the Inner Experience into Words

The dreamer decided to take note of her reactions and spontaneous associations. While she was drawing the rusty bicycle in red color, the dreamer made a connection with her personal power; she felt "rusted" after the traumatic event. Her spontaneous response to the rusted color and her association with her personal power helped her understand what this image meant. Then she drew a red-colored bicycle, with the purpose of returning it to its initial color as above, therefore symbolizing the personal power she was taking back.

Step #3: Identifying the Existential Message

In this case, it is worded as follows: *I can take back my personal power; I do not have to conclude that it was completely lost.*

Now let's see more specifically how the nine dreamwork art therapy methods can be used.

Nine Art Therapy Dreamwork Methods

Dream Re-Entry Through Images

Re-entry into a dream using visual arts is sometimes quite appropriate for certain dreams to further explore them and better understand their message. The dream titled *Five suitcases* is a good example: the dreamer sees five suitcases, each one having a different color and hears *"Everything is ready"*. It is pretty clear that the dream invites the dreamer to open all the suitcases to see their content. It would be possible to work on this dream verbally or through writing, but the fact that the five suitcases have different colors suggests an exploration using visual arts.

Using visual arts to explore dreams through re-entry meets the requirements of the active imagination Jungian method. For Jacobi (1983), writing, painting, sculpting, clay modeling and dance actually are forms of active imagination. *They . . . help to activate the psychic depths, to maintain the vital contact between conscious unconscious contents, and to express the emerging symbols in plastic forms* (Jacobi, 1983, p. 58).

Drawn or painted images are not as easily manageable as words. What comes up on paper is a telling tale in itself, which is in fact equivalent to allowing spontaneous emergence of images from imagination, a typical characteristic of the Jungian active imagination approach (Johnson, 1986; Jacobi, 1983). Using the re-entry approach requires the dreamer to be touched by the images when further exploring his dream using visual arts and imagination. The dreamer may also be actively involved in taking action on the completed images, with the intent to change anything that does not work for him. As an example, he may lessen the threatening looks of a character by modifying dimensions, colors, facial expressions, etc.

To change the ending of a dream by means of drawing is another way to use the re-entry approach through visual arts. It is important that the drawing illustrates a satisfying end; rather than magically solving everything, the ending should imply a change of attitude or behavior in the dreamer. To take responsibility for oneself, to express oneself with more clarity, to ask for help, to work on addressing one's needs are all endings likely to constructively support one's personal psychological evolution.

Active imagination basically involves letting dream images unfold beyond the end of the dream by simply witnessing the images that come up on their own in your mind. The clearest and simplest explanations on active imagination are given by Robert Johnson (1986), author and Jungian analyst. He describes it as a deliberate encounter between the conscious mind and the unconscious mind. He says:

> Essentially, Active Imagination is a dialogue that you enter into with the different parts of yourself that live in the unconscious. . . . In your imagination, you begin to talk to your images and interact with them. They answer back. You are startled to find out that they express radically different

viewpoints from those of your conscious mind. They tell you things you never consciously knew and express thoughts that you never consciously thought.

(p. 138)

The conscious "I" is actually the functional part of someone's identity, the part that makes choices and manages to adapt to social reality. The conscious "I" can decide to explore its inner world, that is a priori largely unknown, in the hope of generating more harmony and efficiency in managing one's Self and one's life. Active imagination, along with dreamwork and self-work through art therapy are very effective approaches to achieve this. In the method suggested herein, visual arts are used alternatively with a more conventional verbal active imagination approach.

Application Example

The Eyelid

My son wants to participate in an ultimate fight. I disagree because I do not want him to suffer injuries. I tell him that I agree as long as he does not get injured. I see a cage and two fighting guys. Then I see an injured eyelid.

The injured eyelid image stayed with me thereafter.

Comments

Using the re-entry approach through images, the dreamer starts to draw the injured eyelid she sees (see Figure 2.2). When the drawing is completed, she sees a round-shaped temple with an exterior door, but she does not know what lies in there.

Figure 2.2 ***The eyelid****.* Chalk pastels, 22½ × 30 cm (9" × 12").

She did dreamwork based on active imagination following this drawing. In her imagination, she comes in through the center door. The dreamer feels she is in a dome flooded with light, but she does not know what it is. First, she sees fire and roots, then the face of an old woman through smoke. In her imagination, she asks the old lady what her message is, but she does not get any answer. The old woman just keeps laughing. There is a lot of wisdom in her. The dreamer is looking for something, but she does not know where to go. After asking the old woman to tell her where she should go, she sees tree branches and tree trunks, as well as green, black and dark blue colors. The trees overlap with each other up in the air and she feels safe in this imaginary place. Something is rising upwards.

The dreamer decides to draw that space and these colors. First, she sees a uterus then red-colored splashes expanding and rising upwards. She realizes that the color splashes radiate from her center and have a flower shape (see Figure 2.3). She feels touched by the beauty of her own center. The dreamer did not elucidate the connection with her son and the two fighting men in her dream. They likely are conflicted parts of herself. Nonetheless, the existential message is to connect herself with her own beautiful center.

Figure 2.3 **The flower in my center**. Oil pastels, 61 × 76 cm (24″ × 30″).

Collage

Collage is easy to use for people with little familiarity in plastic arts expression. It is reassuring and requires little technical skill, since magazine pictures are ready-made. The expert on collage and dreamwork is certainly the Austrian psychologist and art therapist Johanna Vedral, who wrote a book on the subject in 2017.[4]

To illustrate a dream by means of collage, gather pictures representing specific figures from the dream in order to recreate the dreamlike atmosphere. Of course, the dream will not be reproduced exactly as it was experienced – a rarely possible endeavor anyway – but you can collect enough pictures to reflect the essence of the dream and get closer to the dream's primordial image.

As a SoulCollage© facilitator myself, I experienced the SoulCollage© dreamwork method from Seena Frost (2010). SoulCollage© is about creating collages on small cards (12.5 cm × 20 cm (5″ × 8″)) illustrating different aspects of oneself, including sub-personalities, archetypal figures, important persons or mentors of our community and personal guide animals. It is then possible to choose decks of cards reflecting different life issues to use as tarot decks. She mentions it is possible to make SoulCollage© cards about dreams (2010). After experiencing SoulCollage© for my dreams, I found out that the small size of these cards allowed me to retain only images that are essential to a dream, which requires refining the collage gradually in order to progressively grasp the dream's essence. This progressive refining process resulted in me clearly identifying the dream's message once the collage was completed.

Before finalizing a collage, it is advisable to try various placement patterns before gluing the pictures, placing them next to each other in different arrangements. Displaying pictures differently on paper might allow unexpected meanings to arise, as in the next example. Trying different arrangements will help you realize that the pictures seem to have a mind of their own and you will feel where they fit in relation to one another. Some pictures will be rejected while others will become central. Just keep playing with them until you are fully satisfied with the outcome, then glue them down. Be mindful of any reactions generated during this work.

Once you have collected pictures and fitted them together on a large sheet of paper, you might want to take a picture of it for your dream journal later on.

Artists' Materials

For magazine pictures, you might want to collect boxes of images for future use, separating pictures of human beings, animals, landscapes, plants, various objects and places. Keep precious pictures of people of all races, of dreamy illustrations and the ones you find particularly evocative. They might eventually be put to use. You can also subscribe to Internet sites offering stock image banks with free usable pictures.[5]

In addition to magazine pictures, all kinds of collage paper with or without patterns may be used: silk paper, construction paper, newsprint paper, tapestry paper, retail patterned paper, music paper, etc. Additionally, you may create a background using pencils or paint, and arrange the pictures on top.

Putting the Inner Experience into Words

When the collage is completed, it is time to take note of any spontaneous reactions to what happened during its creation, any reactions to the whole process, to all specific images as well as to the pictures that were rejected, in other words to anything that happened during the collage process including the finished product.

If you want to explore further, you can go on with the identification approach to certain images or a dialogue with some of the collage figures: human beings, animals, monsters and even objects. If the identification process is used, let's identify to every aspect of every image. For her part, Seena Frost (2010) suggests identifying to each part of all images using words like "I am one who . . .". This makes it easier to perceive you are in touch with *a part of you* and not with your overall personality. Ideally, the identification process is in written form.

Identifying the Existential Message

Finally, don't forget to summarize the existential message in a brief, clear and precise sentence reflecting your current reality. To facilitate this, just ask "If this collage could tell the dream's existential message, what would it say?" This simple question should help you find the message.

Application Example

The following is a dream from an author, Marie-Johanne Lacroix, who reflects about her experience with the writing process.

My Stone and Glass House

I am standing in front of my house. The first floor is made from solid stone and this comfortable house is a place where we can seek refuge and feel safe. Made from glass, the second floor is like a huge verandah opening onto the natural surroundings. That floor overlooks the environment and from there I see everything, and everybody can see me.

Dreamer's Comments

About the Selected Pictures

I looked for that house in magazines and on the Internet. I finally realized that I had to paste down two pictures, because that house probably was non-existent in the real world.

When I saw a picture of a small stone house, I had a sense of joy and comfort. It triggered the same emotions I had in the dream, in other words a place to seek refuge. I even like the curtains on the closed windows.

Choosing pictures for the glass floor of the house was not that easy; they were too large and improperly fit the picture for the first floor. I had to cut another picture to create the second floor with a glass space flooded with light.

About Her Initial Reactions During the Creation Process

I feel divided, just like the house. There are two movements that do not really fit together. I love the two parts of the collage: the lower one where I turn inward on myself and withdraw within myself, and the top one where connecting to other people and living on the lighted second floor feel nurturing (see Figure 2.4).

Figure 2.4 **The stone and glass house.** Collage from pictures, 11½ cm × 19½ cm (4⅝" × 7¾").

I can easily relate to this in my life. It has something to do with my work as a writer. I write to withdraw within myself, deep within my emotions and my own life, oblivious of the pressure felt near other people.

When my work is published or I read my text aloud, I have exposure and visibility. When I think about that while I write, it makes me want to hide behind the words, to control the writing process and to put a stop to what seeks to emerge. I have difficulty in making these two writing aspects fit, given they interfere with each other.

The whole image helps me feel the two sides of my experience fully, the paradox I can visualize. I can easily relate to that image: one secret side of me and one with exposure. I am at a dead-end. I have the feeling I am caught between two sections of the house that do not fit together.

About Working with the Images in the Collage

I move the two sections around in order to find where they belong. Even if the two floors are arranged one over the other in my dream, I realize with joy that they can be arranged side by side. Thus, they are on an equal basis, standing side by side (see Figure 2.5).

No floor is bearing, no floor is crushed beneath the other. The re-arrangement changes everything. Now I like the overall creation. My

Figure 2.5 **The side-by-side house.** Collage from pictures, 9½ cm × 22 cm (4″ × 9″).

house has two separate wings made at two separate stages using differ-
ent materials, each having their own intrinsic beauty. I like this house
with two wings. I think it is really nice.

This arrangement helps me to better understand my dream and my
need to protect the two sides of my experience as a writer, so that none
should be overrun by the other. I may write in the very heart of my being,
welcoming the words with patience and respect as they come. I can
decide thereafter what will be published, what will be shared and what
will have exposure.

Mask Making

This method is about making a mask representing one of the dream's figures. As a first step, we will make the mask and decorate it; we will then put the inner experience into words, preferably by taking notes of our spontaneous reactions, and finally we will word the dream's existential message.

Art Materials

Different approaches are used for mask making. Of course, you can create a mask using your own face (see later is this section for precautions). Personally, I often use boxes of plaster cloth/bandages from art supply retail stores and a plastic face mask form on which 4 to 5 layers of pre-wetted strips about 2 cm (1″) large will be applied. Ready-made papier-mâché masks are also available and there is no need for plaster bandages, as they are ready to be decorated. On the papier-mâché form, applying a layer of gesso will provide the white surface needed for your art creation.

It is better to use the above mask forms instead of one's own face to create artwork for dreams with impressive figures, such as archetypal ones, given that identifying with powerful figures may cause psychological discomfort. Creating a mask directly on your face can have a very powerful impact, since it looks like you and portrays your own face.

In addition, taking precautions is advised when making a mask on one's own face, because it can cause a claustrophobic reaction. It is not recommended unless you can be accompanied by somebody, ideally a professional art therapist who is knowledgeable about the precautions to take, the safe use of the art material, as well as the psychological impact involved in creating such a mask. If you still choose to create a mask directly on your face, take the time to apply a fat substance such as petroleum jelly on your face hair, your eyebrows and any hairy areas of skin. Make sure your eyes are also protected and you can easily breathe out of your mouth and nostrils. Accompaniment by a trustworthy person is of the outmost importance. Finally, water used for the plaster bandages should never be flushed down sinks, water bowls or water pipes, to avoid clogging. Pouring the contaminated water outside is the only safe way.

When the mask base is ready, you may start painting your dream figure using acrylic, gouache or watercolor if you prefer a transparent look; these are all water-soluble art media. Once the mask base is dry, apply an acrylic transparent layer (called medium) to waterproof and protect the colors. All that is left is decoration, that is adding various three-dimensional pieces like feathers, ribbons, tufts of wool, fabric, fur, collages, beads, sparkles, old jewelry and anything else that reflects the impression from the dream figure.

Putting the Inner Experience into Words

All kinds of events can happen during the mask creation or decoration process. In the same way as for the three-dimensional creation of an object, the most appropriate method will be to take note of any spontaneous reactions to what happened, considering that the mask making and the assembling of decorative pieces will have stirred many significant reactions. Anything that stirred a reaction during art production may have meaning. Here again, you might want to take note of any reaction to the following:

- Different types of lines and shapes on the mask;
- The colors you used and how they impact you;
- The overall impression that is conveyed; for example, a part of the mask gives rise to fears or you like the mask, etc.;
- The art media you used: plaster, acrylic, gouache or watercolor, three-dimensional objects that were assembled, pasted down or attached and especially any sensations caused within you: satisfaction, frustration, wonder, amazement, etc.;
- Any other reaction you might have had during the creative process. The dream's existential message may well arise from these brief notes.

Of course, you can further explore the dream using the Gestalt identification approach or the Jungian dialogue with the dream figure portrayed by the mask.

Identifying the Existential Message

To conclude, just word the dream's existential message in a brief and concise sentence.

Application Example

The following is a dream I had when I was feeling stuck in my Ph.D. dissertation project.

The Statuette of Bast

I meet my thesis director who hands me a statuette of the Egyptian cat goddess Bast. She asks me to open it and divide it in two. Inside the statuette, I can see a small, red-colored thread around the abdomen. The red thread extends up to the mouth then outwardly. When I pull on the red thread, it gets out (see Figure 2.6).

Dreamer's Comments

The topic of my thesis related to my identity as an artist, among others. For the first draft of my dissertation project, I was not willing to share this part of me and my project was rejected. The red color has always related to my identity and pulling on the red thread symbolized freeing my creativity and my identity, to speak my truth about what I wanted. While I did understand the meaning of the dream right away, making the

Figure 2.6 ***Bast, Egyptian cat goddess****. Plaster bandages, acrylic and red-colored thread, 24 × 30 cm (9½″ × 12″).

mask gave a powerful impetus to my belief in what might come out from the core of my being, from my center. The second version of my Ph.D. dissertation project was accepted.

Here is what Rohnnberg and Martin (2011) say about the cat symbol in their book on symbols: Looking through the bright layer of tissue (tapetum lucidum) beneath the feline retina that reflects incoming light, we can learn to track down the hidden parts of ourselves in the dark landscapes of our psyche, without qualms, in order to bring them into the light of day. (p. 302)

Clay Sculpture

As clay is a natural and easily malleable material, awareness will be raised from the shaping of a dream's figure or object with the hands since touch generates powerful sensations and associations. The fact that we create with our hands, and that our hands can only create in accordance with our individuality, will often have psychological impacts that will help us understand the dream's existential message. A young woman in her forties had the following dream after her recent return to school.

Application Example

The Woman with Gears

I briefly see a woman with gears around the waist (see Figure 2.7). *I know there was a lot more in my dream, but the image I saw upon waking up was the one below. Although I saw that image in the span of a few seconds, it remained strong and very clear.*

Dreamer's Comments

Upon waking up, the following thoughts ran through my mind:

> *I have been working with my partner for the last 8 years in a business involving his own trade, whereas I myself pursued studies in art. We both often referred to the expression "Our fingers are stuck in the gear train" to describe this business we have built and are trapped in. Personally, I am definitely not involved in a profession that suits me and I have felt locked in daily life for a very long time, until I decided to go back to school.*

Figure 2.7 ***The woman with gears***. Natural clay, 18 cm × 10 cm (7″ × 4″).

> *I had that dream following my first art therapy class. Upon waking up, the following question ran through my mind: Despite all the efforts made to change my life, do I feel like I am still trapped in another gear train?*

Existential Message

When I gave shape to the statuette using clay, the above question naturally arose again. Given that the gears are around the woman's waist, and considering I am that woman, I realized that I had become the gear train. I am at the core of what will make things happen. I am the revolving machine that causes movement and change. I finally have taken control of my life. I have felt deeply comforted by that thought.

Storytelling

In dreamwork, the storytelling method allows us to unleash our imagination, and helps us distance from our dream on an emotional level. Sometimes, identifying the dream's existential message is easier this way. To write a story, we will start off with a ritual phrase like "Once upon a time . . .", "One day, when . . .", then draw inspiration from the places, characters and actions in the dream to create a story. I suggest involving mythical figures and magical objects, and even witches and dragons. Describing and exaggerating the importance and the role played by the characters, the places and the issues can help reveal more clearly the dream issue. A cabin becomes a castle, a cat turns into a lion. . .

Jill Mellick (1996) offers many suggestions to turn a dream into a fairy tale. She suggests giving a name to each significant element in a dream, to add the words "always" and "never" throughout the story, to use as many qualifiers and adverbs as possible, to give a title we might have found intriguing as a 6 year old child, as well as to write the story using the past tense, as opposed to using the present tense for a dream. No need to create a long story; one or two pages are enough, but we may write more if it feels inspirational.

Once the story is completed, you can use the brief analogy method to find the dream's existential message: *If the story was an accurate portrayal of something I feel in my life, what would it tell?* Here again, it is important to relate this to one's life as precisely and concretely as possible. Your story will likely offer a few valuable clues about the context the message applies to.

You can also use drawing, painting or collage for one or several scenes of the story, which has the advantage of adding visual stimulation to the storytelling process. Proceeding with a drawing of 3–4 scenes of the story is close to the four-steps dream method (see Chapter 1).

To complete the artwork and if further clarifications are needed, it is possible to work on images using one of the three typical written methods: taking note of spontaneous reactions, identification to and dialogue with a dream's figure (see the Introduction in this chapter). That will validate the existential message implied in the written story, which should be worded in a short, concise and precise phrase.

Application Example

The following dream is from a young woman:

A Troubling Date

I dream that I am going to a romantic date with Mr. Marc Hervieux (!!). My partner, Max (in real life), is driving me over . . . in the car, there is tension in the air. We keep silent. While Max seems to display a total disregard, I know he feels hurt. Our daughters are on the back seats. I suddenly realize that I forgot to change clothes and to wear perfume. I am wearing oversized canary yellow jeans, a navy and white striped sweater as well as high heel sandals. When I realize that I neglected to properly prepare myself, I start getting uncomfortable. I keep telling myself that there is nothing to worry about. Max continues to show disregard. He drops me off in front of a supermarket. He is preparing to leave but I cannot bear to be dressed like that. Then I tap on the car and ask him to stop, which he does a few meters further. I get back in the car and we leave to return home. Then we go through unofficial paths, alleys, rear parking lots. Max drives recklessly. The car skids over the gravel ground all over the place. As the car collides with a parked car, I urge Max to leave right away, making sure no one has seen us.

Then I'm at a car dealership. I want to rent a car. Two customer service attendants take care of me. One offers me a family doctor at the expense of the dealer, who also happens to be a gym trainer (?!). I am perplexed and skeptical about this proposal. The other one then proposes to change my car for a family van, which I refuse. I want to keep my car and I just need to rent another one at the moment. She shows me the benefits of the van, like the folding benches to accommodate the whole family for sleeping, but I adamantly refuse.

My Story About the Dream: The Young Indecisive Woman (see Figure 2.8)

Once upon a time, there was a village bordering a gigantic kingdom very far from here, where a young woman lived with her husband and their two young daughters. Even if their lives offered a fair share of minor

*Figure 2.8 **The young indecisive woman.** Watercolor and ink on watercolor paper, 46 cm × 61 cm (18" × 24").*

challenges, they lived a rather peaceful existence, until the day when a letter turned everything upside down. Written by the prince himself, the letter invited the princess to a ball organized by the king to find a contender for his son. The letter immediately created great turmoil in the relationship. The husband, indignant at such an invitation to a married woman, was only more insulted when his wife argued that she could not turn it down.

"Such a request by the prince himself cannot be ignored! It definitely is a case of mistaken identity. I will attend the ball and this will be an opportunity to rectify the situation."

So, when the day finally came, the husband got his wife and children on board his carriage to take his wife to the ball. On the way, the woman discovered with horror that in the haste of the preparations, she had forgotten to put on the skirt she had made just for the event. For fear of showing up for the ball as poorly dressed, she wanted to ask her husband to turn back. But seeing his scowl, she thought it best not to do anything about it and tried to convince herself that all this was a mistake and that, whether dressed appropriately or not, she had no chance to marry the prince! However, when she reached her destination, she was panicked and begged her husband to take her home so she could change clothes.

Finding that his wife seemed to attach great importance to her looks, he realized that her coquetry might hid a secret desire that the prince falls in love with her. As a result, his smouldering anger escalated. On the way home, he was handling his carriage so abruptly that he knocked over and broke the stalls of a few merchants hoping to benefit from the tourism traffic generated by such an event. Anxious to go home for a change of clothes, the woman urged her husband to rush back home non-stop.

Once she was dressed, it became clear to the woman that she could not go so far as to ask her husband to take her to the ball a second time. Then she decisively went to the blacksmith, who provided cattle boarding, to ask him to provide a carriage that she could drive to the castle. Upon arrival, she was greeted by the blacksmith's two daughters. Of course, they had heard of the invitation sent by the prince, because this had caused a great stir. Suspecting the reason for her presence in their home and driven by jealousy, they lied to her saying that their father was unfortunately absent for a while and that they did not know the time of his return. Upset, the young woman started thinking, but the two blacksmith's daughters began to throw so many questions at her that she was unable to focus on finding a solution. Did not she want a cup of tea? Did she wish to buy fresh eggs or feet from the pig that was slaughtered the night before? Somewhat dazed by all this, the woman finally came to her senses and firmly refused every offer before leaving.

Saddened by her ill luck and wearing her most beautiful finery, she took a seat on the stump of a large fresh-cut tree to reflect on her situation. Where did this irrepressible urge to go to the ball come from? Why so many road blocks along the way? Secretly, as unlikely as it may seem, did not she dream that the prince actually falls in love with her? Did not she want that romance to propel her out of her routine life? Now, if she gave in to her desire, it would cost her what was most dear to her in the world: her family. Was this sacrifice really worth it? How could she be happy without them? Her husband was not a prince, but a good and kind man, with great qualities of heart, who loved and cherished her. Would it not be easier to go back to her close ones and forget that mad infatuation? Yet her attraction for adventures and the unknown was definitely stirring deep in her heart. Could she accommodate this need otherwise than by breaking up her marriage? Indeed, now that the seed had been sown, the young woman was well aware that this attraction would haunt her for the rest of her life. How to involve the one she loved tenderly in her taste for strong emotions that can get her carried away with exhilaration and quench her thirst for novelty? How to be content with the quiet and orderly life that her husband wants?

All night long, elbows on her knees and hands under chin, the young woman mulled the question over, unable to find a single answer. At sunrise, a strange and mysterious phenomenon occurred. As the first rays of the sun began to dawn, the young woman felt her body fade into the wood of the tree stump. Without knowing why or how, her skin quietly merged with the fibers of the tree trunk. She realized that her indecision was about to turn her into a wooden statue, freezing her to the spot forever. Overwhelmed with emotion for a moment, she made one final attempt to find answers to her questions, but she quickly realized that it was just too late. She soon turned into a wooden statue, lost in her imaginings forever.

Ever since, hundreds of people in search of answers to existential issues stop at the statue, and many grasp a great truth after having observed it: it is better to make a choice and risk being mistaken than to stand idly and end up being paralyzed.

Existential Message

Instinctively linked with elements of my waking life, this dream became surprisingly consistent after having written the story. First, I have been aware of my taste for adventure and novelty for a long time. Although daily routine is necessary and provides security at times, I personally find it demoralizing. I like having big projects and dreaming big as well as making plans to carry them out. I like to think that willingness and creativity make it all possible. However, there is the opposite polarity in me: I find security and stability comforting. My partner is an entrepreneur and finds fulfillment in his daily big projects so that when he is at home, he just needs peace and quiet. So, it makes things complicated for organizing our weekends to make sure it is a win for everyone! For a long time, I felt resentment against my partner and his inaction on weekends. I was constantly questioning whether I would find happiness with someone else. However, every time I had such thoughts, a big part of me did not see separation as being a solution.

About a year ago, I discovered art therapy and I made it my major life project. Becoming an art therapist is a goal I will do my utmost to reach. But now I am facing important professional choices if I want to walk the path inspired by my spirit and my enthusiasm. I am presently in a sabbatical year to pursue my education in a field I am passionate about. Now, by the end of the school year, I will have to decide whether I resign as a tenure teacher to face the unknown and job insecurity, or I prefer to get back to a comfortable and safe job knowing I would feel more at ease.

I keep mulling the question over: should I leave or go back? I know that as long as I sit in a state of indecision, I will feel paralyzed and frozen like a statue. My dream actually ended when I refused the offers from the customer service attendants (the blacksmith's daughters). It is the end of the story, a figment of my imagination, that led to the existential message I got: it is better to make a choice and risk being mistaken than to stand idle and end up being paralyzed . . . While that message says a lot to me, it does not provide answers to my question, it indicates that no good comes of harboring fears and doubts.[6]

Sandplay

Sandplay is another original and effective method that can be applied to dreamwork. This therapeutic method was introduced by Dora Kalff (2004), a Jungian psychotherapist. Using a box of sand of a specific size,[7] children or adults create an imaginary world in the sand, using miniature figurines.

Materials Used

The miniature figurines used for sandplay include characters, household pets or wildlife, birds and insects, natural objects, houses, buildings and other man-made structures like bridges, fences, wells, etc. They are placed into a sandtray box during the sandplay. The size of the sandtray box is important so that the player can cover the whole creation in a single glance. From a psychological standpoint, the sand box offers the advantage of having specific limits as well as a reassuring symbolic frame of reference where one's inner world can be circumscribed. The sand can be wet if one wishes so. Painted in blue, the bottom of the box will look like water and allow lines to be traced out, for example rivers and lakes, while playing in the sand. If a box having the right size is not available, one can create a similar one using a container that is large enough and filled with fine sand. Then you simply need to get miniatures depicting characters, landscapes or objects from the dream.

Ideally, one should seek professional support from a sandplay therapist[8] or an art therapist using sandplay, because they usually have an extensive collection of miniatures and they are knowledgeable about dreamwork using sandplay. However, to carry out dreamwork on your own, here is the process. First, use your hands to sculpt sand so as to create hills, rivers or other landscape features. Then position the miniatures that call to mind the dream's ambiance. Once you are pleased with your creation, use the process described below for your dreamwork. This approach through process and dialogue with the figurines was taught to me by my art therapy teachers from California, Lillian Rhinehart and Paula Engelhorn (1987, 1982), and I frequently use it as part of sandplay therapy sessions.

The Six-Steps Process Approach of Sandplay

1. THE SANDPLAY STORY

First tell the story associated with the sandplay and/or write down what is happening. When the sandplay is about a dream, just tell or write the dream story.

2. IDENTIFYING A HERO

Pick up a miniature to represent the sandplay hero and another one for the character that will represent you. If you are not included in the dream, pick up a miniature you identify yourself to and include it in the sand box. It will serve as a witness of the dream.

3. IDENTIFYING THE THEME OR THE ISSUE RAISED WHILE DOING SANDPLAY

Here, the theme/issue raised while doing sandplay will be worded: *Is there anything upsetting about the sandtray? Is there something that does not suit you completely?* Once the theme/issue becomes clear, it has to be summarized in a short and clear sentence. What if everything feels right in this imaginary world? Well, just put into words the sense of well-being felt during sandplay and the dream. But it is rarely the case.

4. SEEKING SOLUTIONS

Afterwards, the character who represents the sandplayer is moved around to meet the other figurines and ask questions in order to better understand the theme at play, or to identify which figurine can help find solutions to the problem.

The last step is about changing the configuration of the sand box and the miniatures so as to reflect the solution. To do this, you may want to remove or add figurines, to alter their arrangement or the sand patterns, and so on. It is important to make sure you are totally comfortable with the new configuration of the sandtray box.

Finally, the existential message will be put into words. Typically, handling the sand and the figurines as well as altering the sand patterns are enough to clarify the dream's message. The creation of such an imaginary world effectively promotes self-awareness about what is going on in our inner world.

Application Example

The Woman in the Torrent

I am attending a class in a university lecture hall. Multiple people dressed in original, brightly colored garments are also participating. I leave the room with one woman. We are going to her place. I am in awe of the apartment's décor, but we are promptly out of it and go eat out. We end up in a wilderness environment with trees, a stone path and a torrent we are walking along. The woman walks in front of me. Her green clothes are very unique and catch my eye. I also see a man who is carrying a heavy bag effortlessly on his back. He makes me think of an immigrant. All of a sudden, the woman who is with me falls into the torrent. There is a man in the water. He manages to grab her but she squirts right out of his hands and nearly drifts away. But the man finally manages to grab her. Looking at the scene, I feel helpless and I have a strong urge to assist with the rescue. I end up holding out a long pole to her. I am the one to get her out of the water. She is naked. She shows me that she has a groin injury. We go back to her place. It feels like she is not naked anymore. She is going to change her wet clothes. The door is left open. I see it is a very modern black and white apartment. I am staying outside. Then I find myself with two or three women wearing a head scarf. I realize I am wearing one over my beret. I pull on it from the back to slide it over. Two of the women share heartfelt kisses. These women seem to know the one who is with me. We are waiting for her to go eat out.

Dreamer's Comments

Here is how the dreamer experienced each step, after recalling her dream and retelling it.

1. Identifying a Hero

I take a first step by selecting which figurine represents me. It takes time for me to find which one is appropriate. I finally pick up an African woman who looks like a warrior. At first, I think, if anything, that this is a masculine warrior. But I am pleased to find out she is a woman. I like her. With this new heroine, I am going to meet with the other figurines in the sand box for the purpose of finding how my wounds can be healed.

2. Identifying the Theme or the Issue Raised While Doing the Sandplay

What I find so intriguing and troubling about the story that unfolded during the sandplay process is that the woman I rescued from drowning has injuries. I also feel uncomfortable about the female figure wearing a head scarf. As soon as I look at her, an impression of submissiveness comes to my mind. There is an African woman carrying wood on her head. This scene brings to mind carrying a burden, being overworked. I find that these aspects of the world I created are disturbing.

3. Seeking Solutions: The Hero Meets Other Figurines

We will first meet the man figure to ask him what I should do when doubt sets in and I feel powerless in certain situations. He reminds me of the creativity and resolve I demonstrated to save the woman who fell in the torrent. Right after, I go and meet the friend who wears nice clothes. I ask her how I can assert myself as a woman. She says she is a part of me who likes nice things and that I already assert myself through wearing original clothes and jewelry even if it looks extravagant. It is significant that I chose a Geisha, a highly refined artist who perpetuates the Japanese traditional arts, including clothing. Then I get closer to the woman with a physical mark who fell into the water; this encounter reminds me how hurt I was in my femininity in my own family where boys always had the final say. She comforts me recalling that I rescued her and I now have every- thing I need to move forward and take charge of myself as a woman. Then I meet the woman carrying wood on her head. I ask her the same question. She tells me that saying "No" is self-assertion as well. Sometimes, I feel overworked and I let myself be overwhelmed with too much work. She reminds me how important it is to enjoy life. Besides, I have been building that strength for a while.

4. Making Changes During Sandplay

This journey brings me to making changes in the sandbox. I first remove the woman figurine with wood on her head. Then I relieve the man of the bag he carries on his back and he returns with the other figurines. The only thing I add is an elf sitting on a rock with an open book in his hands. As I place him in the sand box, I declare that what he is hold- ing is the Book of Intuitions. I keep forgetting at times that the path/ voice of intuition is a part of me and that I am guided when I trust my intuition.

I pause to reflect on this new configuration. I realize that all the figu- rines have their back to me since they are looking to the torrent and the stone path along the water. I feel as though I am standing by and watch- ing what is unfolding before my eyes. Then I make the decision to move the figurines around. I arrange them in a circle and observe the result. I find it pleasing. Now feeling more involved, I feel the need to change the ending. Instead of going out to a restaurant to celebrate, I organize a circle of women for the purpose of sharing what was experienced.

5. Identifying the Existential Message

Taking a closer look at the steps of the sandplay, I realize that it involves many defining sides of myself. I first become aware that figurines I removed from the box have left a trail, a memory in the sand, and that they embody parts of myself. The man who carries a bag effortlessly on his back refers to my capacity to carry heavy work tasks. As for the woman carrying wood on her head, she reminds me that I can say "no" to a new file that I consider less relevant to me. I am struck by the size of the Geisha who is a dominant figure in the sandtray. She represents a feminine side to my personality that I developed and feel comfortable with: my clothing and my adornments may reflect my desire to make up for my family's attitudes towards women. However, the woman who has fallen in the water is small in stature. My understanding is that even though I still fight to achieve recognition as a mature woman within my

*Figure 2.9 **Sandplay: the woman in the torrent.*** Sandtray box and miniatures, 75 × 50 × 7 cm (30" × 20" × 3").

family, it does not impact me as much as before. With regard to the elf holding the book about intuitions, he is a small and important character who represents unconscious knowledge and sheds light on my intuitive powers. The warrior, for her part, somehow summarizes my position as a woman who stands for herself and is ready to move forward. The world that was created in the sandtray has been engraved within me and is held as an unforgettable memory.

The dream's message is that despite the hurts associated with the fail-ure to recognize women in my family of origin, I now have full confidence in the woman I am and my capacity to say "no" when it feels appropri-ate. I no longer need to carry heavy burdens just to prove myself. And I can now be a part of the women's circle.

Embodying the Dream

This method requires us to stop and feel the residual physical sensation from the dream then to express it through dancing and painting. Dancing allows spontaneous body language, letting the body move in response to what is expe-rienced in the dream; the body will simply express the sensory trace generated by the dream. While doing this, we just need to pay attention to the physical sensation generated by dancing and what is being experienced through body expression. Then we use painting or drawing to trace on paper what is felt through dancing. You can also do the opposite: first make a drawing of the dream's global feeling and then express it through dancing.

Gendlin (1986) did dreamwork using what he called the felt sense or bodily sense. For him, the inner certitude about the meaning of a dream came from the bodily felt sense, in other words the body response to a dream. More specifically, his clients were instructed to make different assumptions about the meaning of their dream, then look at their body's response to each one, since the body has instinctive knowledge of the truth. He gave the following example: when we scroll through our mind in search of something we neglected to bring with us somewhere, we make a number of assumptions for which the conclusion is "*No, that's not what I am seeking*", until we put our finger on it and there is no doubt anymore. As for the meaning of a dream, it is possible to get the same inner certitude. That is completely consistent with my experience about the existential message of dreams.

Application Example

Dreamwork was done on the nightmare *A Fight between Athena and Aphrodite*, through *embodying the dream*. The dreamer was a participant in one of my workshops about art therapy and Greek goddesses taking place on the sea front. Greek goddesses essentially are archetypal representations of different feminine energies affecting the women's psyche. Athena is an ancient Greek goddess associated with warfare and handicraft (male polarity), whereas Aphrodite is the Greek goddess of love and creativity (female polarity).

A Fight Between Athena and Aphrodite

I am attending a group session for women about dreams and Greek goddesses. I feel good and I await the arrival of my sister Louise who decided to surprise me and show up two days into the session. We are instructed to dress as goddesses. Another woman then comes in, but she does not clearly understand the instructions and turns into a man. I am very embarrassed that she does not understand the instructions and so interferes with the group. She makes noises with her mouth that send shivers down my spine. I drag her away, but she still manages to escape to return to the group of women. She constantly changes forms, but always turns into a very bad guy.

I woke up and felt very afraid. I had a fast heartbeat, but strangely enough, I had an orgasm.

Here is how the dreamer worked on that nightmare by embodying the dream:

Figure 2.10 **Integration of feminine and masculine energies.** Watercolor pencils, 20 cm × 25 cm (8″ × 10″).

Dreamer's Comments

After dancing and drawing huge characters and doodles in the sand on the beach, I sat down facing the sea and made sounds. I was trying to focus on making female-type high-pitched sounds and male-type low sounds. Then, I walked towards the sunset. I crouched down, facing the sun, to watch the sunset. I sat this way until the sun went down. I was dazzled and amazed by what I saw. The combination of sun and water reflecting on the sand filled me with joy. I experienced the harmonious integration and meeting of all these forces: the water, a feminine element and the sun, a masculine element, were in perfect union.

The day before, I had also made a drawing that truly depicted what I felt in my body (see Figure 2.10). There is a subtle man's face with moustache on my left wing.

Existential Message

I understood that the masculine and feminine sides of me were conflicted, and that a reunification of polarity occurred in my body.

Color Exploration

Sometimes a dream features a specific color that is related to an object, a person or is simply present by itself. Colors usually bring an emotional response in the dream; the meaning will be influenced according to the image they are associated to (Hoss, 2005). As for me, I believe that dreams are essentially feelings reflected into pictures, especially if colors are present. So, if we simply explore a color, we address a significant aspect of the dream (Hoss, 2005). Identification and expression of emotions have a major impact on personal transformation, hence the importance to take a closer look at colors.

To do so, spread the color on the paper sheet and see which associations come out of it. A color you never use in your drawings and paintings or for clothing will be particularly significant. Ideally, several shades of the same color will be used and explored with several art media that may each have a different impact. In this case too, let us ask ourselves where, when and how this emotion or feeling is felt in our daily lives. It should be noted that emotions can be specifically identified, for example anger, fear, joy or sadness, whereas feelings are something broader, and often include a number of vague or general sentiments such as love, well-being, tension, and so on.

Application Example

The following dream is from an adult student working on the career choice theme.

A Night-Time Show

I am in a park and it is winter. It's evening and it's dark, but the park is lit. I am attending an acrobatic act. A girl in a gold sequin evening dress is about to make a show on large metal trapezes. It looks like a quite perilous act. I fear for the girl. She goes straight up into the air and manages to go from one metal structure to another, and then to set foot on the ground. I then decide to try my luck. I am feeling unsure, but I manage to do it. I decide to go back home. I live in a house near the park. I am walking in the snow in the darkness. Suddenly, a tall black wolf with golden eyes glowing like fog lights shows up in front of me, staring at me. It jumps joyfully into the snow and searches with his snout, makes snorting sounds. Fear is gripping me. The wolf is not threatening, but I know wolves are temperamental. I am a few blocks away from home. I am trying to keep a low profile as best as possible to remain unnoticed. He does not pay attention to me and I finally get home.

Dreamer's Comments

At the beginning of the dreamwork, I first became aware that other than the gold-colored dress of the trapeze artist and the wolf's eyes, all the other features were in black and white. So, it became appropriate to explore the gold color, and I knew right away how to proceed. For the initial drawing, I traced the contours of the young woman and the wolf using a lead pencil. Then, using a paint brush, I applied white glue to the inner surface of the dress and the animal's eyes, and I sprayed a generous layer of golden glitter over it. As the result perfectly reflected the color in my dream, I immediately felt pleased with it.

After observing the gold-colored dress of the young woman, I wondered what it represented. Then I wrote down the answer that came up: "The gold color represents elegance, glamour, a formal show outfit that is stunning. It has the appearance of wealth, the chic that catches the eye and raises applause. It is the golden look of a queen, a star that dazzles and amazes the audience. The trapeze artist must be careful and thoughtful. She must pay attention to dangers ahead and be present in the moment. She cannot see anything else, not even the crowd holding its breath. She will look at them once the danger is gone. Besides, the danger seems much worse than it really is."

Then I focused on the wolf and wrote down: "The gold-colored eyes of the wolf represent clairvoyance. It is the light that makes it possible to see everything, even beyond the visible and the present. It is a light that shines from within with a brightness beyond description. It is sacred, extremely powerful and carries a mystery beyond me, an impenetrable mystery that makes me confused when I try to solve it. The wolf has tremendous power, but still is temperamental. It carries with it a destructive potential as much as a creative potential. For the moment, it's a loner and it is no worse off. Impetuous and temperamental, it does not live for anybody else but himself. However, I am very eager to tame it and make it an ally as well as a partner. I feel that we would form a team in perfect harmony and complementarity."

I started thinking about the connections I could make between this dream, my achievements and my waking life. I immediately realized that it was related to my professional life and the important decisions I would have to make shortly. Back to school for over a year, it felt like I had found a path that I was passionate about and made me feel like my professional situation had a chance to come back to life. However, that implied financial choices that could make me feel dizzy (yet the trapeze artist was not dizzy!). Moreover, it required courage and self-confidence that faltered on occasion. At this stage, while I could easily make connections with my situation, I was still not sure I understood the existential message of the dream. I felt connected to the trapeze artist who was about to jump off into the void, probably looking for recognition and applause. I was pretty sure that the wolf referred to great inner power. I instinctively knew I had to focus on the gold color glowing from within, because the flashy gold-colored dress would quickly lead to emptiness, and its radiance would lose interest.

I decided to go for in-depth exploration of the gold color. I started looking for any gold-colored art supplies at home. I found a wood pencil, a small acrylic paint tube and gold dust. As it was far from being enough, I thought of looking for gold-colored pictures in magazines. While I was searching, I became aware that this color was uncommon and difficult to find. Using a few pictures and the art media I had in hand, I created a first piece that looked like a barren moonscape. When creating the art piece, I felt good and in control, but when I stepped back to look at the result, after running out of all the gold-colored materials I had, I felt a sense of loss and sadness. Here is what I wrote down then: "Inaccessible landscape, barren desert. I wish I could understand what this gold color is all about, an unfathomable mystery carrying an eternal message. Do I belong here? Do I have such a power within me? How can I connect with it? The answer to the last question emerged immediately: "Just follow the wolf. He knows the way." However, I knew in my heart that the wolf would refuse to come with me in this barren desert landscape. Then I felt sad and helpless.

In everyday life, this feeling often occurs in connection with my thinking about my professional future, and it is twofold. Although I am conflicted by the investment and the financial risks that this new professional alternative implies, the dream is clear. The danger seems much worse than it really is. By proceeding carefully and thought-fully, the trapeze artist can easily get around the danger. In addition, and this is where the problem lies, I fear that my inner light will not be strong enough to dazzle people and that people will remain indif-ferent. I am also afraid to aim high, to overestimate my ability and my value as well as scared of failing in my career shift . . . I also fear that people will not recognize my value and will not clap for me at the end of the show . . .

As I reflected back on that, I felt sadder. Looking at my art creation, I felt disappointed. I thought to myself that if only there was a gold-colored background, there would not be such a sense of loss. Visualizing the collage on a golden background made me feel good. So, I put on my boots and my coat to go buy the needed materials. At the store, I had to stop myself from buying each and every gold-colored item. It felt like purchasing precious goods, and the more I picked up gold-colored items, the more I regained confidence. Back home, I cut up the items from my

Figure 2.11 **Gold color artwork**. Gold paper sheet, gold-colored sequins, golden dust, acrylic paint and cut-up magazine pictures, 30 cm × 35 cm (12″ × 14″).

initial art piece and I glued them to the gold-colored background (see Figure 2.11). After adding a few more items, I felt very pleased with it. Now, the landscape looked lively and beautiful and I knew that the wolf would definitely be pleased to stay with me. More importantly, I knew it represented a sacred space within me. While the mystery of that space remains unsolved, it lives inside me and for me, and reassures me that anything is possible.

Existential Message

I realized I was successful by following my instincts and listening to my inner voice as well as taking over the task to get everything I needed without cutting corners, and that's how I was going to find my way.

Healing Rituals

A healing ritual can be developed for a group or for oneself, as I was taught by Alexandra Duchastel, a fellow psychologist and art therapist. It allows us to promote a transformation of the collective consciousness towards well-being, to facilitate a life transition or to better anchor a desired change of consciousness in oneself, or within a group. To use this approach, it is essential to use some of the elements contained in a dream to design a ritual promoting such a transition or change. The ritual serves to amplify the positive or potentially transformative aspects of a dream and to make them more effective.

Application Example

Mrs. Duchastel developed two rituals that are used in her art therapy groups: a group ritual and a self-healing ritual. They are as follows.

First Example – The Following Dream Inspired a Group Reliance Ritual

In 2011, I was mandated to officially open the first Art Therapy Conference hosted by the Université du Québec en Abitibi-Témiscamingue, in Rouyn-Noranda, Québec, Canada. The conference theme was "Quests for identity: the background for the art therapy approaches"(Quête d'identités: La toile de fond des art-thérapies). I did not have a clue what presentation I would make. I was racking my brains about the original contribution I could offer to an event bringing together leading international experts from different schools of thought.

One night, I had the following dream about a character from the prehistoric novel authored by Jean M. Auel (2014).

I am alone in the depths of a dark and wet cavern. I'm cold. In the distance, I see the sparks of a fire dancing around in the night. In my right hand, I am holding a small piece of rope that I am fiddling with, wondering what use it can serve, given its small size. Suddenly, in the depths of the cave, I hear movement behind me. I'm scared. I'm afraid of the dark, of the invisible world, of what is moving and sighing in the shadows. It is a human sound and yet dehumanized. I realize that the sound actually comes out of my own mouth, but that several other beings are responding in the lonely night. Not quite sure why, I throw the small piece of rope in the shadows, in the lonely night. After a few minutes, it comes back like a boomerang, but I notice that it is now longer. I throw it again, and it comes back even longer. I finally realize that we are several to languish in the shadows, punished for having cut the thread that connects us. Subsequently, the world of my dream changes and I end up on a beach in

Portugal. It is a sunny day and I watch the fishermen pull out their wet and tangled nets and lay them on the hot sand. Together, in a slow silent dance, the fishermen try to untie the knots.

Dreamer's Comments

Upon waking up, I felt that these isolated people in the shadows who are barred from the clan represented the art therapists belonging to different schools of thought who fall apart and lock themselves into exclusionary definitions of the profession rather than uniting. The healers of the imaginary, the creative therapy professionals, the art therapists and the psychologists using art for mediation all draw from the same source, but everybody wants their own corner. In doing so, some of them have become disconnected and disengaged from the community.

This art therapy conference proposed a shared reflection. Every participant was bringing his own perception of things, coming with the intent to meet with a favorable response for his own vision or, on the contrary, to draw stimulation from new perspectives. However, a sense of trust and belonging to the group needed to be built for our argumentative differences to become nurturing.

My dream offered the cornerstone for the creation of a reliance ritual involving an experiential co-creation activity that would allow us to move beyond our traditional mode of operation based on rational intelligence as well as to reach out to all participants at the core of their sensitivity, where they recognize one another beyond their different viewpoints. So, I just had to amplify the piece of rope image in order to create an atmosphere conducive to fruitful sharing.

I recently had been initiated to the ancient art of felting by a friend of mine, Danielle Bissonnette, actress and Jungian storyteller. In fact, felting was the first textile of mankind, the oldest artifact dating back to the Neolithic period (6500 BC), in the days when survival depended on collaborative interaction from all members of a clan. I found fascinating how flexible and strong yet stable this non-woven textile was (no tearing, no fraying), given it is made from wool fibers that otherwise are fragile and easy to break.

The Reliance Ritual

The 120 conference participants received a little bit of carded wool and were invited to rub it between their hands. As the animal fibers were rubbed more and more together to form a string, an ancient knowledge emerged from the collective unconsciousness and took us back to archetypal memories then to the current sharing experience, beyond words, theories and definitions. Rubbing the wool fibers together for the purpose of turning them into a solid string served as a reminder of Jason's deter-mination, who had set out on a quest to acquire the Golden Fleece in order to take back his father's throne. Just like Jason, the art therapy community was about to embark on an impossible quest.

Thereafter, participants were asked to use felting to join all individual strings in order to form a long piece of thread, that is Ariane's thread. To do this, they had to stand up and go next to each other in an intimate collaborative effort. The participants were thus invited to a creative act through body movement. In less than half an hour, all participants are connected through a long thread weaving all along the different rows. We were now connected through our similarities and to each other like climbers that are roped together.

Comments from Mrs. Duchastel About the Meaning of the Reliance Ritual

From that moment on, all individual experiences shared throughout the ritual help build a coherent and unified group ("close-knit people" as Que-becers say) having more confidence in the multi-disciplinarity of its mem-bers. The slightest act of a person impacts all the other individuals and, by changing the perspective even slightly, enables the expansion of the range of possibilities. By analogy, any scientific breakthrough by one of the group members automatically further develops the overall art therapy research. As issues are now submitted for analysis and thinking by all members, the potential solutions found are sometimes surprising and unexpected.

I think the future and the recognition of our profession depend on our capacity to weave the web of art therapies together to create a solidarity network honoring all of its forms. To do this, we urgently need to recap-ture the intelligence of both the mind and the heart to get it over with the turf wars and the quarrels between the different schools of thought.

The reliance rituals and the use of metaphors like the Ariane's thread and the Golden Fleece allow to facilitate the inclusion of our identity viewpoints. Since then, I have done this ritual over and over again in various contexts, sometimes with more than 400 people!

Second Example – The Following Dream Inspired a Personal Healing Ritual: Letting Go and Love

One of my clients is suffering from a complex autoimmune disease and chronic fatigue since childhood. The following personal dream inspired a ritual I now use for myself and my clients. Since my client and I have been practicing this ritual, we both are much healthier.

Marianne and the Weight of the Ancestors

I dream that I am lumbering down. I am trying to walk, but it feels like I have boots of lead. All my muscles strain and my whole being is engaged, but I am not moving forward. Feeling discouraged, I turn around and suddenly become a passive observer of a scene taking place on a small island in the Greek Archipelago. I am looking at Marianne who is walking down a rough road that slopes down toward the village's marketplace. As her mother, her grandmother and her great-grandmother did before her, she carries green olives from her olive grove in large mesh bags. Although she is young, Marianne looks like a weary, exhausted and very sad elderly woman. For having been dragged around in the mud, the bags filled with olives carried by Marianne are now as large and heavy as watermelons.

At the marketplace, Marianne is unsuccessful at selling her olives that are clogged with mud. She employs different techniques to remove the heavy clods of clay from the olives. Finally, what works best is to throw them against the wall.

Dreamer's Comments

I was struck by how clear I was with the woman's first name in my dream, since I had no close acquaintances like her in real life. The etymological dictionary indicated that the name "Marianne" came from the Virgin (Mary) and her mother (Anne). I also found that it was derived from the name "Myriam" that dated from ancient Greek times and meant "the loved one".

Marianne wants to break the cycle of hate and ignorance. She is the one who loves in spite of everything. However, she no longer has the strength to love herself, because she helplessly carries the sorrow of her ancestors on her shoulders.

I understood that obviously the ultimate solution to build back up my energy was to cut old ties and let go of these dead weights. Referring to the language of the birds, the word "olives" spontaneously reminded me of "0 lives" (zero life). But I could not bring myself to give up on and ignore my ancestors who suffered. So, it merely remained for me to turn the issue over to a force larger than myself. The following ritual was thus developed.

Ritual: Letting Go and Love

At the start of a silent walk in the wilderness, a small clod of clay the size of a small olive is sculpted, to depict any individual whose energy I carry within myself. During the walk, the clod is symbolically loaded with love and wishes for the sufferer (this may include myself). Halfway, in a place of power, the small clay sculpture is entrusted to Gaïa/Mother Earth.

The intention is said out loud, with full awareness and ideally in front of witnesses. Depending on the intensity of the emotion, the clay sculpture may simply be hidden in a tree hollow, buried under a pile of moss, glued to the rocky wall of a canyon, thrown into the eddies of a waterfall or deposited along the riverbank. Each time an individual deposits clay, he recovers some of his energy that can be used for his own healing.

Comments from Mrs. Duchastel About that Ritual

Neurosciences help us understand why healing is hardly ever immediate. Repetitive symbolic gestures are often required to anchor a new experience. That's why healing rituals are effective to the extent that they are performed on a regular basis and with full awareness. Freeing oneself can be managed one step at a time over many life cycles.

That ritual can be performed individually as well as in groups.

Notes

1. For a complete description of these basic art therapy dreamwork methods, see Hamel, J. (2021). *Dreams, art therapy and healing: Beyond the looking glass.* New York: Routledge. Or in French: Hamel, J. (2017/1993). *Rêve, art-thérapie et guérison: De l'autre côté du miroir.* Montreal: Québec-Livres.
2. These steps were first published in English in Hamel, J. (2021). *Dreams, art therapy and healing: Beyond the looking glass.* New York: Routledge and in French in Hamel, J. (2017/1993). *Rêve, art-thérapie et guérison: De l'autre côté du miroir.* Montreal: Québec-Livres. However, they are worth repeating here since they serve as a framework for the nine following methods.
3. For a more complete Gestalt identification method, see Hamel, J. (2021). *Dreams, art therapy and healing: Beyond the looking glass.* New York: Routledge. Or in French: Hamel, J. (2017/1993). *Rêve, art-thérapie et guérison: De l'autre côté du miroir.* Montreal: Québec-Livres.
4. You can visit Clare Johnson's website for examples of dream collages and explanations in English. Johanna Vedral's book is in German language: Vedral, J. (2017). *Collage dream writing: Geschichten aus der Tiefe schreiben.* Wien: Verlag punktgenau. https://schreibstudio.at
5. Here are a few examples of websites offering such images: https://search.creative commons.org; www.denisebossartebooks.com/background-image-gallery/; www. dvcreators.net/where-can-i-find-free-stock-photos/; www.getty.edu/art/resources; https://reikilifestyle.com/category/dphoto-galleries/; and this is an annotated list of websites with free images: http://skinnyartist.com/CHEat-sheet-for-finding-free-images-online/
6. Author's note: she did become an art therapist!
7. The sandtray box size is 75 cm × 50 cm × 7 cm (30″ × 20″ × 3″).
8. See the Canadian Association for Sandplay Therapy (CAST) at www.sandplay.ca, for a list of members.

3   Nightmares as a Source of Individuation

Introduction

Nightmares are among the most important dreams one can have: they represent parts of oneself facing a major challenge. They typically occur at a time when one needs some inner resource that was denied or repressed; the challenge comes from the unavailability of that resource. The intense emotion one feels reflects how significant this resource is, the amount of repressed energy as well as the importance of the existential message for one's current life.

Some researchers believe that the function of dreams is to simulate dangerous situations to help us face them in waking life and to teach us how negative emotions can be handled. According to Revonsuo, a Finnish researcher (cited in Arnulf, 2016), that theory is based on the fact that 60 to 77 percent of dreams in young adults involve threats. Researchers also found that dreams involve on average twice as many negative emotions (fear, anger, shame) as positive ones (joy, happiness, pleasure) (Arnulf, 2016, p. 28).

Personally, I consider that nightmares feature parts of ourselves we are afraid of or that we learned to consider as negative, shameful or unacceptable. We disconnect from them in order to survive more effectively in our social and cultural environment. Their integration into our personality helps us become more complete, wholesome, harmonious and happy. That is how Jung (1993) defines psychological healing. Therefore, dreamwork about nightmares is one of the most powerful tools to be used for the purpose of personal evolution, a process Jung called individuation.

The individuation process concept is one of Jung's major contributions to Western psychology, according to Marie-Louise von Franz (2006). Individuation pursues some secret goal, and that is Self-realization, the archetype of wholeness. The Self always aims at directing one's individual evolution for the purpose of self-realization and full and complete maturation. It is both the center of the entire psyche and an inner guide that can mostly be grasped through dreams. According to Louise von Franz (2006), "something hidden is at work, is geared to an objective and generates a progressive psychological growth. It is a self-realization process, a self-actualization process"(p. 334).[1] Individuation comes first through integration of the shadow, in other words the inclusion of all the repressed sides of oneself into the psyche.

DOI: 10.4324/9781003124610-4

The Self comes as typical symbols in dreams, art and imagination, such as a circular shape, a mandala, a square shape, a diamond, a rose, a golden ring, a pearl, a chalice, a wheel, a cross, or every time a quaternate occurs (Johnson, 1986; Jacobi, 1965). The Self may also feature a king, a wise man, or a religious character like Jesus, Buddha. . .

Nightmares offer a unique opportunity to work on our individuation process, given how significant their message is. They are so important that whenever I am lucky enough to have a nightmare, it is welcome! I know the message will be of great help for my personal growth.

A Few Definitions

Nightmares are symbolic dreams which can leave unbearable feelings of fear, terror, anxiety or other intense painful emotions upon waking up. Nightmares can also contain threatening situations, feelings of imminent loss, grieving, fear of the world coming to an end or any intense emotions such as sadness, disgust, rage, humiliation, betrayal, guilt and helplessness. These emotions often come with disturbing physiological reactions like difficulty in breathing, sweating, a racing heart or physical pain.

In a typical nightmare, the dreamer experiences a situation where he is chased hostilely by a monster, a terrifying animal, a thief or an individual with the intent to kill him, or where he feels helpless because of life threatening situations like suffocation, falling down through the air, drowning, incapacity to scream or call for help, paralysis, loss of control, feeling lost or humiliation like being naked in public, failing an exam and other similar threats.

In addition, nightmares can depict traumatic life scenes, as for war veterans, natural disaster survivors, motor vehicle accident victims, armed attack victims or other critical situations such as childhood traumas.

Furthermore, nightmares can be differentiated from simple bad dreams and night terrors. The difference between a nightmare and a bad dream is the intensity of the sensations or emotions felt by the dreamer. The typical unbearable feeling of fear, panic or terror coming with nightmares causes the dreamer to wake up whereas bad dreams feature daily anxiety and concerns, and do not necessarily cause the dreamer to wake up. To the extent that the dreamer tries to find a solution during sleep, it will only be a bad dream, but if no solution can be found, it will turn out into a nightmare, according to Hadfield (1977), a specialist in nightmares.

Especially prevalent in children, night terrors are marked by unique, uncontrollable and terrifying images occurring at the onset of the sleep cycle, even before the REM (Rapid Eye Movement) stage that is usually associated with dreaming. Morris (1985) believes that night terrors are related to developmental processes. Children wake up screaming in terror, unable to remember any part of their dream.

However, Isabelle Arnulf (2016) believes that adults also experience night terrors and she differentiates them from nightmares. To her, night terrors contain imminent death threats where the dreamer's typical response is to run away from bed; she gives examples like drowning, a ceiling that falls in, snakes . . . In nightmares, however, there would be assault scenes that would not necessarily be life threatening.

Since many parents do not know what to do when their child wakes up from night terrors and nightmares, a short guide is included at the end of this chapter and there is a section for therapists dealing with children.

The Seven Types of Nightmares and their Function

In my professional practice, I observed seven types of nightmares, each having a different function. They will be reviewed in more detail and illustrated with examples. Most of them suggest a variation of the self-regulating function: *revealing childhood traumas, expressing intense unconscious experiences, resolving emotional shocks, projecting missing resources, illustrating unresolved inner conflicts, integrating traumas*, and *premonitory nightmares*. Each type of nightmare and its function is reviewed below.

Revealing Childhood Traumas

I observed that many adults have vivid memories of recurring nightmares from childhood. Nightmares symbolically depict painful aspects of their experience from childhood, for example sexual or physical abuse. Abuses that have been forgotten or repressed are reflected in dreams through symbols. When nightmares are elucidated during adult life, they are indicative of how some aspects from childhood were experienced and how the adult's waking life is still impacted by them.

Example of a Typical Nightmare about Traumas from Childhood

The Drawer (Recurring Dream)

I am dreaming that I am lying down, but my head is enclosed in a drawer.

This person was wondering why she felt today like she didn't want any children. In her childhood, she felt she had to mature faster and be the mother of her own mother as well as of her numerous brothers and sisters. The drawer reflects how that situation caused her to feel trapped during childhood.

Expressing Intense Unconscious Experiences

When intense and painful emotions are felt by a dreamer who did not become aware of them in waking life, they can be made explicit through a dream by exaggerating their expression or the feeling experienced while dreaming. Any emotion needs to be expressed at least within oneself by welcoming it as opposed to repressing it, to avoid causing inner pressure.

For Morris (1985), nightmares are parts of ourselves that are trying to emerge. She sees nightmares as catalysts that compel us to recognize feelings or urgent emotional needs that are crying out for attention. She believes that nightmares serve the following purpose:

> To keep us honest with ourselves; they prevent us from ignoring the things we intuitively know but don't want to be true. We all have an inner guide that can't be conned and that will, if more subtle forms of communication fail, scare us half to death to get our attention.
>
> (p. 233)

Corrière and Hart (1978), in turn, consider that nightmares reflect repression and avoidance mechanisms of our true feelings and that they disappear when we learn to fully and clearly express our emotions in waking life or while dreaming.

*Example of a Typical Nightmare About Expressing Intense
Unconscious Experiences*

The Outhouse in the Fields

I am sitting down in an outhouse in the middle of the fields. There is a small square wire window in the door at my head, and I am sitting to have a pee. I see a bolting horse that is galloping; it has drool in the mouth and mad eyes. I can't do anything because I'm peeing. It tears off the wire with its teeth but cannot stick his head through the window. I wake up in a panic.

Dreamer's Comments

I have just left my husband. A few days after the dream, I went for a walk on Mont-Royal with my sister. Suddenly, a galloping horse from the Royal Canadian Mounted Police arrives and it is bolting like in my dream; it is heading right towards me and I jump into the ditch to avoid it. I panic.

In her dreamwork, the dreamer became aware of how much she was always terrorized by men and the reason for this inner experience. The dreamwork on her nightmare will be detailed at the end of this chapter (see Figure 3.3).

Resolving Emotional Shocks

Nightmares occur following painful and disturbing events in our lives. Through dreaming, we try to make peace with them and to integrate the experience in the psyche for the purpose of eventually being able to restore our inner balance. Typically, the dream follows major losses: bereavement, particularly mourning a child, separation or divorce, loss of important relationships with friends or with relatives as a result of conflicts in the family of origin, grief at the onset of a serious illness, etc. Although conscious in waking life, these feelings are intense and generally felt over a long period of time. Therefore, they come back repeatedly in dreams to help us deal with them.

Example of a Typical Nightmare About the Resolving of an Emotional Shock

---

The Explosive Device on a Steep Hill

I am on the edge of a very steep hill where workers from a company are doing experiments. They are going downhill, carrying a flammable product in their hands. I am observing as they are going down. They get to a wall and crash against it. The explosive device falls to the ground, and they too fall down and die. The company does one, two or three experiences of this kind. In the end, the owner says "I am experienced, I will go there and make it work".

I take a few steps back to make sure I don't block the road because the roller skates on my feet are somehow blocking the way, but I am not moving, I stand still and observe what's going on over there. The owner sets on his way with his device, going down right at the middle of the hill, at high speed. He gets to the wall, climbs to the top of it with incredible strength and then falls back to the ground with the explosive device. When he reaches the top of the wall, I hear a cry of death, a cry from beyond the grave. I am stunned as well as everyone else around. When the man crashes, I only see his black device on the ground, I don't see the dead man (See Figure 3.1).

I woke up feeling troubled by that cry of death. I keep hearing that terrible cry again and I feel deeply troubled every time.

Comments

Through art therapy dreamwork, the dreamer became aware that the black object was the very image of death. The words that came to her mind were the following: "*It is the image of a person who hits a wall for having given it all.*" These words reminded her of her husband who had

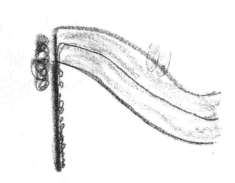

Figure 3.1 **The explosive device on a steep hill.** Dry pastels, 46 cm × 61 cm (18" × 24").

Alzheimer's disease, but also of her son who died at the early age of 50 and of three more close ones who all passed away in the last 15 months. The cry of death referred to her son in particular, given that nobody expects to die after one's child, even though he was seriously ill. The dream caused her to go through the intense grief of losing her son and allowed her to go a little further in resolving that emotional shock.

Projecting Missing Resources

Nightmares where we are chased by a monster, a killer, or a scary figure are a clear example of this dream type. What we are chased by is a part of ourselves seeking recognition and integration into our consciousness.

For Von Franz (2008), nightmares are associated with the shadow archetype. Shadow often manifests in dreams as a threatening and unwanted character who is of the same sex as the dreamer. It depicts a part of us that is repressed and denied; we will keep being afflicted by that part until the time it is integrated into our consciousness, recognized as a part of us and used as a new resource. Once it has been assimilated, this part of us will prove to have positive aspects.

Nightmares restore balance by making the dreamer aware of an important aspect of their experience, particularly emotions of fear and anger. Kaplan-Williams (1987) considers that the main purpose of nightmares is to teach us to cope with fear and thereby to take our personal power back. Indeed, if we are afraid of any figure in a dream, it is because we have projected onto it our own aggressiveness or our capacity to defend ourselves. If we take charge, we get back our capacity for action.

Jung (1970) believes nightmares come from not paying enough attention to a part of us in our conscious attitude. If it carries enough energy, it will emerge in a dream and even wake up the dreamer due to its intensity: "An unconscious compensating factor will intensify when it is vitally important for the orientation of consciousness" (p. 216–217).[2]

For Hadfield (1977), monsters, for example, personify intense feelings of fear, rage, sexual desire or other feelings that we refuse to recognize as part of us, and give an objective reality to them.

For Laberge (1985), nightmares express the anxiety that arises when facing a situation in which our usual behavior patterns are ineffective. A recurrent dream most likely indicates a need for a new way of dealing with the situation depicted in the nightmare.

Example of a Typical Nightmare About Projecting Missing Resources

The following dream is about the suffering artist in me:

Undergoing Surgery "for Science"

I am lying on two stretchers at the same time. A woman dressed in white performs a surgical procedure on me. She has already removed my right eye and the brain area behind the eye, because when I open my right eyelid, it is empty, there is only one black hole. The woman has put these parts in the other "me" on the seconds stretcher. I think to myself that I have been split into two. Then the woman will do the same with the inside of my mouth, on the right side. I am pinned to both stretchers with small fine pins, like a butterfly. The woman says, "It's for science".

Comments from My Dream Journal

The association with the missing right area of my brain instantaneously reveals the meaning of the nightmare, since I consider that the right brain is clearly related to the artist in me! That dream is telling me that because of my work as a university professor, which is "for science", I do not allow much time for my artwork, and that makes me feel like being split into two.

Ultimately, that dream and a few similar ones told me that I definitely had to find a way to nurture the artist in me, since that resource is currently an unmet need.

Illustrating an Unresolved Inner Conflict

For Laberge (1985), nightmares result from an unresolved conflict that the dreamer does not want to address in waking life. Sub-personalities or complexes may be conflicted in the psyche without the individual being even aware of them. In such a case and when the conflict has an impact on our immediate life circumstances, a nightmare may happen to warn us about our inner turmoil, which will then allow us to start working to resolve the conflict.

For Freud (2016/1900), nightmares reflect sexual conflicts; each dream comprises the fulfillment of repressed desires. When a desire is highly unacceptable and if it is so strong that the forbidding may be overridden, then a nightmare occurs. This type of conflict may cause physical sensations in the belly and other areas of the body.

Example of a Typical Nightmare: Illustrating an Unresolved Inner Conflict

The example mentioned in the previous chapter will be used for this purpose:

A Fight Between Athena and Aphrodite

I am attending a group session for women about dreams and Greek goddesses. I feel good and I await the arrival of my sister Louise who decided to surprise me and show up two days into the session. We are instructed to dress as goddesses. Another woman then comes in, but she does not clearly understand the instructions and turns into a man. I am very embarrassed that she does not understand the instructions and so interferes with the group. She makes noises with her mouth that send shivers down my spine. I drag her away, but she still manages to escape to return to the group of women. She constantly changes forms, but always turns into a very bad guy. I woke up and felt very afraid. I had a fast heartbeat, but strangely enough, I had an orgasm.

Comments

While she worked on her dream, the dreamer realized that two identity energies were conflicted inside of her: the feminine side of her and the masculine one. As she gained clarity, she paid attention to this inner conflict and worked on reunifying both sides in her.

Integrating Traumas

Dreams about traumas arise as a result of highly disturbing events that are relived in these type of nightmares, and they are generally recurrent. It is the case for post-traumatic stress disorders (PTSD) sufferers, for example.

A traumatic event may or may not lead to a post-traumatic stress disorder. PTSD diagnostics are defined in the DSM V (2013) as follows. There must have been exposure:

> ... to actual or threatened death, serious injury, or sexual violence in one (or more) of the following ways:
>
> 1.   Directly experiencing the traumatic event(s).
> 2.   Witnessing, in person, the event(s) as it occurred to others.
> 3.   Learning that the traumatic event(s) occurred to a close family member or close friend. In cases of actual or threatened death of a family member or friend, the event(s) must have been violent or accidental.
> 4.   Experiencing repeated or extreme exposure to aversive details of the traumatic event(s) (e.g., first responders collecting human remains; police officers repeatedly exposed to details of child abuse).
>   Note: Criterion 4 does not apply to exposure through electronic media, television, movies or pictures, unless this exposure is work related (2013, p. 143).

There must also be one or more intrusion symptoms, including recurrent and involuntary memories (i.e., recurrent nightmares, flashbacks); avoidance of external reminders; inability to remember aspects of the traumatic event(s); fear and negative mood; hypervigilance reactions (exaggerated startle response, sleep disturbance, problems with concentration), among other symptoms.

Dreams about integrating traumas are typical from veterans who re-experience war situations, but they are also associated with motor vehicle accidents, natural disasters like hurricanes, tsunamis, devastating tornados in which we lose parents, friends, our house or when we suffer physical abuse, a life-threatening disease or even a simple surgical procedure.

Jung (1970) refers to these dreams as being "reactive", given their emergence does not enable a self-regulating function or restoration of inner peace. Jung argues that whether we understand their meaning or not does not reduce their effects and recurrence. We must wait for the termination of the trauma stimulus, as he maintains (p. 225). They come into being as a response to objective traumatic life events like war.

It seems, though, that art therapy may help promote the termination of the trauma stimulus. Through art, a step-by-step approach to trauma memories and the intense emotions involved is made possible. Morgan and Johnson (1995) conducted a very interesting experiment to test the hypothesis that drawing nightmares does not retraumatize the client, while the use of written language may do so. They worked with two veterans, comparing the effect of drawing their nightmares with that of writing them in a 12-week intervention. Drawing and writing their nightmares alternated three weeks on and three weeks off.

Both subjects reported a decrease in the frequency and intensity of nightmares during the weeks they drew them upon waking up, while their nightmares worsened the weeks when they noted them down as soon as they woke up. Obviously, the very small number of subjects does not allow us to generalize such results, but may prompt us to research whether drawing nightmares may lead to a decrease in their frequency and intensity.

Pesant and Zadra (2010, 2006) outlined a technique involving repetitive mental imagery (RMI), where dreamers were asked to alter the scenario of their dream as they please and to repeat it to themselves several times a day. This had the effect of decreasing both the frequency of nightmares and the feelings of distress related to nightmares in post-traumatic stress disorders sufferers. This approach is similar to the methods *positive art* and *four-steps dreams* (see Chapter 1).

Example of a Typical Nightmare About Integrating Traumas

A Bloody Scene

There is a scene where I see a bloody carnage: four or five bandits killed four or five good people. I am a police officer and I am standing on the bloody scene with a group of policemen. I know that the same scene with the same people will happen again. But this time, I know it and I will be able to stop the bandits. As one of my friends arrives, I tell her that she should leave. I tell her what is going to happen and I do not want her to be traumatized by the bloody scene.

Dreamer's Comments

I had breast cancer five years ago. Since then, I frequently dream that I am at risk of death. I felt that this was a life-threatening disease and I am struggling with the fear that cancer will come back. This dream is telling me to stop fueling that fear: this time, I am going to stop the bandits! In the dream, asking my friend to leave is like asking myself to avoid being traumatized by the bloody scene, since in the Gestalt approach, my friend represents a part of myself. My fear decreased afterwards.

Premonitory Nightmares

Premonitory nightmares show us future events that will happen exactly as depicted in the dream. We may not necessarily know that a nightmare is premonitory until it becomes self-fulfilled in reality. Some people recognize a premonitory dream when they have one, and might be inclined to panic when faced with such a nightmare. There are two points to keep in mind: first, alert any people that are affected when individuals in danger are identified in the dream; second, be aware that dreaming about an event does not mean we caused it to happen. There is no use in feeling guilty. This type of nightmare may be considered as a gift, a warning that serves to avoid some danger.

Example of a Typical Premonitory Nightmare

Motor Vehicle Accident

I am dreaming that my friend is involved in a motor vehicle accident at the corner of King and Wellington Streets in Sherbrooke. A truck racing down King Street at high speed smashes her passenger side door.

Comments

The dreamer simply warned her friend by suggesting she pay close attention to this crossroads when driving and even to avoid passing through it for a few weeks. Ten days later, when this friend was about passing through the area, she saw a truck racing down King Street at high speed; she took the time to watch carefully and averted the collision, thanks to the dreamer's warning.

Five Steps to Efficiently Work on Nightmares

I identified five steps allowing us to address a nightmare: steps to soothe challenging emotional issues, then steps for in-depth work and for bringing out the resources. But first of all, I suggest making a *nightmare box* that will serve to "lock in" our nightmares until they decrease in intensity within us.

To create a *nightmare box*, we need a big enough box to store different unruled paper sheets used for drawing or writing down our nightmares. Then we will decorate the outer part with pictures that we like, find soothing or are likely to work as an antidote against the fear, terror and panic feelings that cause us to wake up following a nightmare. This box including the sheets of paper will be kept at our bedside. A dry medium will also be included in the box, for example a set of wood pencils, felt tips or oil/dry pastels.

The five nightmare dreamwork steps are as follows:

Step #1: Appeasing emotions
Step #2: Emotionally distancing oneself
Step #3: Identifying the existential message
Step #4: Turning the nightmare into resources
Step #5: Implementation of the resources

Step #1: Appeasing Emotions

You will start with looking for the area where the painful emotion is felt in your body: is it in your heart? In your chest? In your belly? Is there a sense of fear, horror, terror, panic, imminent threat, an intense feeling of loss, mourning, of the world coming to an end, hopelessness, suffering, powerfulness, vulnerability, betrayal, guilt? Does it go along with painful sensations like shortness of breath, sweating, rapid heartbeats or pains?

Then you will make a quick rough colored sketch of the emotion or the physical sensations using some dry medium. This step is very effective to ease the painful emotions and sensations.

The next step is to start breathing as described below; as a result, any emotions will cool down very quickly. As you inhale, just think the following: "I presently have feelings of fear (or horror, terror, panic or any other emotion that was identified)"; then as you exhale, think the following: "I am letting go of fear (or horror, terror, panic or any other emotion that was identified)". Repeat as many times as necessary, but it usually will not take too long. This technique is inspired by mindfulness meditation (Kabat-Zinn, 2009a).

For example, upon waking up from a nightmare, I was feeling very angry. After a quick sketch about this feeling (see Figure 3.2), I immediately cooled down. I was able to get back to sleep after noting down the nightmare, knowing I could come back to it a few days later to understand what the feeling

Figure 3.2 **Quick sketch about intense anger.** Dry pastels, 21½ cm × 27½ cm (8½″ × 11″).

was related to. It is actually very important not to be satisfied with soothing the painful feeling and to come back to it later to understand what the feeling was about and go on with the next dreamwork steps. Otherwise, the nightmare might come back until the message is understood.

Step #2: Emotionally Distancing Oneself

Now, you will write the nightmare story using the past tense, on separate paper sheets that will be stored in your *nightmare box,* along with the drawing from Step # 1. Wait two days before coming back to it or until you feel ready for more dreamwork. It is only once the nightmare has lost its traumatic impact that you will be able to come back to it and try to elucidate its message.

Step #3: Identifying the Existential Message

When you feel ready to come back to the nightmare, you can use different work methods to elucidate the existential message. The easy starting point is to use one of the amplification methods for the key felt sense in a dream (see Chapter 1). At Step #1, you already identified the feeling and/or the sensation felt upon waking up. Now, you can ask yourself in which context, with whom and where you might somewhat have felt that emotion in your waking life? Do not forget that nightmares aim to bring an unconscious aspect to our attention and that emotions are exaggerated for that purpose: nightmares willingly *scare us to death* to help us becoming aware of a vital aspect in our life, as Morris (1985) puts it. Therefore, your experience in waking life may not be as intense as in nightmares. It may also be something unconscious that you don't even know about.

If the existential message remains unclear after using the amplification approach for the key felt sense, I recommend, given how important nightmares are, to keep on doing dreamwork using a range of different creative methods (see Chapter 1) which will allow you to move progressively towards the understanding of the nightmare's existential message or one of the art therapy dreamwork methods (see Chapter 2). For example, you could do a *re-entry into a dream through images*. This method is extensive and also allows the dreamer to distance himself from the dream figures that would be too "negative" through Jungian dialogue.

Step #4: Turning the Nightmare into Resources

Nightmares aim to bring attention to an inner resource we deny ourselves access to. As an example, are we able to be assertive enough if need be or to set limits and say "no"? Dreams allow us to glimpse into what is missing and what we need precisely to face a specific and immediate situation in our waking life. We might need to change our attitude, or our behaviour to better meet our needs. Rewriting or redrawing a dream in which we change our attitudes or our behaviours will allow us to tap into such a resource. Step # 4 is the one that comes closest to the intervention technique involving repetitive mental imagery (RMI) from Pesant and Zadra (2006), which is effective for trauma dreamwork.

Step #5: Implementation of the Resources

Any dreamwork about nightmares will only be worthwhile if we take action by translating it into practical use and incorporating it into waking life. Taking action through small reasonable steps will play a key role in translating the nightmare into resources and preventing it from recurring. It is the most effective means to ensure real change in waking life and in nightmares.

Application Example for Steps #3 and #4, for Effective Dreamwork on Nightmares

The dreamer who had the nightmare titled *The Outhouse in the Fields* decided to explore it further using a series of creative methods. She had had that nightmare many years before, always remembered it and understood it was about her relationship with her mother, which did not feel very positive to her. She decided to do in-depth dreamwork about it since it stuck in her memory as being significant. But let us first recall that dream and the dreamer's comments about it:

The Outhouse in the Fields

I am sitting down in an outhouse in the middle of the fields. There is a small square wire window in the door at my head, and I am sitting to have a pee. I see a bolting horse that is galloping; it has drool in the mouth and mad eyes. I can't do anything because I'm peeing. It tears off the wire with its teeth but cannot stick his head through the window. I wake up in a panic.

Dreamer's Comments

I had just left my husband. A few days after the dream, I go for a walk on Mont-Royal with my sister. Suddenly, a galloping horse from the Royal Canadian Mounted Police arrives and it is bolting like in my dream; it is heading right towards me and I jump into the ditch to avoid it. I panic.

The dreamer used this series of creative methods to work on her dream long after its occurrence:

I decided to make a doodle (see Figure 3.3).

I see this as a fetus and it reminds me of my mother's pregnancy. She was running away from danger, pregnant with me, throwing up in the car, had motion sickness and wished only one thing, that is to die.

Figure 3.3 **Doodle.** Drawing pencils, 22½ cm × 30 cm (9″ × 12″).

To me, this doodle is about rebirthing to the woman I am and this is inspired by the two left circles that look like nipples to me. I also see a heart shape and I write down: "Rekindling a woman's heart".

Then I decided to change the ending using the Positive Art method in order to continue my dreamwork:

> *The horse tears off the wire and calms down, then I pet it (I feel uncomfortable like if I have no choice and the horse does not deserve it), but then I can finally have a pee with intimacy.*

The horse represents terror, violence and my father when he was furious with me like a bolting horse, and acting temperamental, getting upset with me instead of getting mad at what was actually making him angry, and hitting me till I urinated in my panties. Perverse pleasure. There was no safe haven for me because my temperamental father was beating me up at home, and I did not feel safe out of my house either. I then realize that in my dream, I protect myself by seeking refuge in the outhouse where the horse cannot come in. The encounter on Mount-Royal embodies the dream in reality to help me overcome my fear. Indeed, I later go to a stable to groom a horse and feed it. I even taste its feed grains.

Then I closed with a Haïku:
Peeing in the outhouse
The bolting horse at the wire window
I am protected

Existential Message

In the context of my separation, I was becoming vulnerable again since I could meet men again, and I had always been terrorized by them. But I now feel protected and I am no longer as vulnerable.

The next day, the image about the horse tearing off the wire mesh comes back to my mind and I decide to change the ending of the dream again, because I am not really satisfied with it. I decided not to pet the horse, to let it calm down by itself. This is important because I am not responsible for its violence and it is not up to me to take action to help him cool down. In my imagination, the horse starts to trot in front of me and to strut about in order to show off, and it seems to invite me to ride it, which would mean for me to welcome a new intimate relationship . . . Time will tell. "Rekindling my woman's heart" should help me deal with men differently.

Comments: In that dreamwork, by becoming aware of how much she has been terrorized by men and by understanding the origin of this terror, the dreamer's childhood trauma was alleviated. The dreamer recovered a part of herself and took over her power to choose.

So, using these simple but powerful methods can greatly help us cope with our nightmares and appease ourselves. In fact, the quick sketch is so effective for that purpose that you may be tempted to stop working on the dream and forget about identifying its existential message and the hidden resource. However, it is by identifying the hidden resource and using it that you will ensure that a nightmare never returns. Nightmares are a most unique gift as, like all other dreams, but even more so, they will help us free ourselves from our deepest distresses. As Jung said: "The patient becomes self-sufficient through self-creation"[3] Jung (1993, p. 124).

Guidelines for Parents and for Child Therapists: What to Do with Nocturnal Terrors and Nightmares of Children and Toddlers

> Ask the monster if it wants to be your friend and play with you.
> Waggoner & McCready, 2015

Guidelines for Parents

For children who have frequent nightmares, please keep small paper sheets, colored pencils or felt tips near their bed. Also keep a *nightmare box* for the child to store their stories or pictures about nightmares. Ideally, let the child decorate his or her own box.

Let's Differentiate Between Nightmares, Bad Dreams and
Night Terrors

The difference between a nightmare and a bad dream is the intensity of the emotions felt by the dreamer. The typical sense of fear, panic or terror coming with a nightmare causes the child to wake up, whereas the bad dream features daily anxiety and does not necessarily cause one to wake up.

DEALING WITH NIGHT TERRORS

Typical night terrors among children are marked by unique, uncontrollable and terrifying images occurring at the onset of the sleep cycle, even before the REM (Rapid Eye Movement) stage that is usually associated with dreaming. Morris (1985) believes that night terrors are related to developmental processes. Children wake up screaming in terror, unable to remember any part of their dream.

Most children do not wake up during night terrors, and it is not advisable to wake them up anyhow. The terror response of a child is more of an anxiety-inducing situation for parents than for the child himself. When a child wakes up during a terror stage, it makes total sense for parents to provide support. As night terrors come without images, it is advisable for parents to give reassurance by being present and caring. Regardless of age, offering the child his favorite comfort object or cuddly toy helps. Remember that denying the terror felt by a child would do no good; however, tell the child that you are with him and that he is now safe.

DEALING WITH NIGHTMARES

For children, aggressions or threats are very real, and affirming they do not exist will only increase feelings of panic. It is better to work with a child's imagination. As an example, invite the child to describe the monster or villain and to tell you where it is. Is it hiding under the bed or in the wardrobe? Depending on where it is located, ask what could be done to stop the monster from scaring him. For example, could he be put in jail underneath the bed? Could he call for his favorite hero to come rescue him and send the monster or villain away from him? You might want to put up an imaginary fence (or a real one if available) to prevent the monster from escaping the wardrobe. The solution must come out of the child's imagination so that it can provide effective calming effects.

Subsequently tell the child that you will write down his nightmare for him and that it will be stored inside the nightmare box.

If the child cannot calm down, ask him to make a drawing of his solution; at the most, wait until the next day for this. Drawings give a concrete and visible reality to the imagined solution and therefore often produce an effective calming effect. The child is reassured because the visual representation confirms that his fears are real, thus preventing denial, and providing evidence that they have been expelled from him by transfer to paper. In research by Simard and Nielsen (2009, cited in Pesant & Zadra, 2010), children were given the suggestion to change nightmares through drawing, and it was proven that it resulted in a substantial decrease in the frequency of nightmares and the associated sense of helplessness.

And finally, it seems children can often learn to become lucid while dreaming by being told: "You only see the monster when dreaming, right? So the next time you see the monster, remind yourself that you must be dreaming. Ask the monster if it wants to be your friend and play with you" (Waggoner & McCready, 2015, p. 150).

Guidelines for Child Therapists

Rarely do child therapists know how to work with nightmare issues. This is why this guidance and the following case history may help.

Dreamwork for troubled children, in particular about nightmares, can be very beneficial to inner confidence and security. The guiding principle is the same as above; it is about valuing the children's perception and working with their imagination to find a symbolic solution. When possible, engaging them to make drawings of the threats and the imaginary solutions will indeed have greater impact on your work. The following work involved a young 5-year-old boy suffering from enuresis and was realized in three sessions over a period of six weeks. This example will help you learn how to proceed.

An Example from Mrs. Édith Bergeron, Psycho-Educator

She performed the following wonderful work sessions:

I was working with a five-year-old child who frequently wetted his pants both at school and at home. Every time he told me about a nightmare, I suggested to write a story about it and he was willing to do it. The following is a dream about the Virgin Mary:

The Yellow Sword

I am at the school's daycare service. I am taking part in a sword fight. I have a yellow-colored sword. I see the suspension bridge and Mary who is standing on it. She is pushed off the bridge by a villain. I do not like that, I feel afraid.

I used the following dreamwork approach:

> After writing his dream, I read it. I asked him how his dream would end if he could make up a different ending. I pointed out that it had to be a happy ending because the superhero of the dream was himself.

He spontaneously said, *"I will throw the villain off the bridge."* Looking at me silently for a few seconds, he then added "No, the whole family, including my cat, will throw him off the bridge".

He made a drawing about this new ending.

The next week, I used an anchoring approach through reading a book about inner strength and making up the new ending for his dream.

A few weeks later, I was informed by the school instances that the young boy wetted his pants were now rare occasions, and his parents confirmed that he was also doing better at home.

I am convinced that the dreamwork played a crucial role in helping the young boy take back his power over the situation. During the dreamwork process, he paid attention and focused on his art creation. Once it was over, I saw pride in his eyes and his body language: he was sitting upright and was listening intently. He felt like a superhero . . . and what he had done felt important to him.

Notes

1. Free translation.
2. Free translation.
3. Free translation.

4 Lifelong Dream Journals Methods

Introduction

People who start writing down their dreams and doing dreamwork often do so over many years. However, those who revisit their dream journals are relatively few. Cluttered with a lot of boxes full of dream journals, many simply consider getting rid of them! Yet, there is a lot to be learned from them. It would be a shame to waste such valuable information: our dream journals virtually tell the story of our psychological life. This is actually the point of this chapter that identifies methods allowing to draw some wisdom from them. The ones suggested in this book are inspired from art therapy and imply using two-dimensional art media (drawing, painting, collage, world map, writing. . .) or three-dimensional ones (sculpture, leather or fabric crafting, assembling various objects, clay. . .), from specific themes to be found across all the dream journals.

The art creation or representation of dreams using these methods can be followed or not by dreamwork to elucidate their message. However, the mere presence in our environment of objects created or represented from dreams will have an impact on our psyche.

It can be very enlightening to work on dreams that we had long ago. A lot can happen with past dreams. First, we can understand them instantly by reading them over again, by the sole effect of the passing of time. It is easier when we have noted what was going on in our lives at the time of our dreams, but this also happens just because we generally remember who we were a year, two years ago, or at the age of 20, 30 or 40 years. Second, working on past dreams will likely allow us to identify an existential message related to our current state of mind. As a certain internal coherence is maintained over time, a message will also have relevance for who we were at the time we had the dream and even for the present moment. Here are 11 methods to be used with all of your dream journals.

Eleven Methods for Lifelong Dream Journals

Dreamworld Map

Some dreamers regularly see the same places again in their dreams, whether it is known locations, imaginary places, places from their childhood, sites where

DOI: 10.4324/9781003124610-5

they traveled or rooms in their house. I suggest drawing a geographical map of these places, especially if they often come to mind. This is not the case for everyone, but sometimes a dreaming life has this peculiarity. As an example, I know that in my childhood, I was going back to my magical land night after night. Unfortunately, I have no recollection of that. All I remember is that one day, around the age of 12, I realized that I had stopped going back to my imaginary land at night. I experienced that as a real loss and a deep feeling of dismay and mourning. Imagine what fun it would have been to map that.

Some regularly dream that there are new rooms in their homes. Here again, it would be interesting to browse their dream journals to list all the new rooms added over the years, then review what they refer to in their story, what new parts of themselves they bear witness to.

In her book *Pathway to ecstasy* (1990), Patricia Garfield proposes a very refined version of this method. She suggests including our dreams in a Tibetan Buddhist-inspired mandala, placing them in the four directions: north, east, south and west, or at the center. She draws on the five basic deities of the Tibetan Buddhist philosophy to organize her own dreams in a mandala. She suggests using images; the dreamers who made their mandala in this way felt that they better understood who they were. This approach is in keeping with the spirit of the methods outlined in this chapter.

The *dreamworld map* is a method that draws on Mrs. Garfield's approach in a more concrete way. For the dreamers who always return to a fairly specific set of places, the dreamworld map will offer a limited number of places, which will make it possible to review them in order to identify the constants. Thus, it becomes easier to make connections between a dream and what has been experienced during a day. Therefore, it is, in itself, a truly original method for grasping what is going on in our psyche; it puts forward another very colorful and more concrete way of understanding our experience. As an example, do you dream of a specific room in your house when you have experienced sadness during the day? Do you dream of your house's surrounding garden when you feel creative? There are endless possibilities, and it will be up to the dreamer himself to discover them, by drawing the map of these places and taking note of the constants.

Application Example

The following example is about a man who has always dreamt about the farm from his childhood.

My Dreams at the Farm from My Childhood

I lived on a farm until the age of 18. There were animals, fields, woods, a barn and a stable and just below, sheds and a large house full of rooms as well as nooks and crannies. There were also boundaries that I sometimes crossed to go to a neighbor's land, experiencing discoveries and adventure into uncharted territory. When I find myself at the farm of my childhood, I know right away that my dream will relate to my deepest identity. Over time, I have become aware that in times of change or uncertainty, I happen to return to one of the paths leading to a neighbor's land. For example, I see myself going to the Fontaine's land, a place I wanted to explore when I was a kid. I see myself walking in the fields and arriving at the barbed wire fence. In my dream, I can see myself crossing this fence and finding myself on the other side, seeing new things that were never there in my childhood. It is a double pleasure to go back to that place, reliving the excitement and making new discoveries of things I did not know of, such as a new building never seen before as a child. In short, my dream brings a sense of exhilaration at the discovery of a new pathway. When I wake up, I know I am looking for a way to deal with the situation I encounter in my waking life. Whenever I discover a new place as I explore, it is typically because my dream literally offers a different perspective on the situation. This example is one among many.

We were surrounded by five neighboring lands accessible from many trails. In many dreams, I travel these paths. Upon waking up, I find it interesting to question why I explored one path rather than another. In addition to the content of the dream, I can ask myself: Why did I prefer going to the Fontaine's land this time? As a child, these neighbors had a training track for horses. It was a place charged with mystery. Sometimes, I would get closer to the fence and look that way. Crossing the fence and going to find out something new in a dream makes me relive that sense of wonder.

On the contrary, every time I was dreaming that I was near the fence of the Bathalon's, I felt insecure. Indeed, the Bathalon's were neighbors at the back of our land who had developed a coffin building company. When a dream goes in that direction, I rarely ever cross the fence, because I prefer to observe and walk along the land. I wake up with a feeling of discomfort that may relate to events in my waking life that cause these same feelings.

Two other examples of neighboring trails and dreams come to my mind. In my youth, I thus happened to cross the boundaries of the Murphy's land, our front neighbor, which is bordered by a creek, a fence and thickets. This boundary was very attractive because of a scrapyard for old cars that would be disposed off into a bush by the neighbor, right next to the creek. My brother and I typically went there to get into the cars, without asking permission, of course. I sometimes went back there in my dreams. Why there? Maybe to regain a sense of power. Going from one car to another and imagining myself driving them gave me that sense when I was a kid. Maybe I need that in my life at the moment

I am dreaming. Precisely at the time when I'm running an organizational operation that requires me to take charge!

A fourth example relates to the boundaries with a neighbor and friend of my father called Ashley. At the time of his retirement, my father often went to his house for logging, where he was also producing what he called "new soil", that is to say land-clearing. That was not really fun for the children who also had to participate in the stump removal and the clearing of stones, given these terms clearly refer to pain in arms, back pain and perhaps anger. Dreaming about this land from Ashley causes me to experience rather peculiar moments when I look back to both the pleasure of returning to these places and the pain of having to obey my dad following his decision that the timing was right to produce "new soil". Dreaming about these moments sometimes points out to me that I have mixed feelings in the face of an upcoming situation: my interest in accepting a new job, but also the fear of facing unexpected outcomes and regretting my initial choice.

Now a few words about our last neighbor: M. Ouellet, who offered a path to freedom for me. In fact, as soon as I crossed the fence, I ended up on my way to the village a few kilometers from our farm. As I was often alone with my young brother and there were no friends our own age in the neighborhood, it was the road into the city and society. When

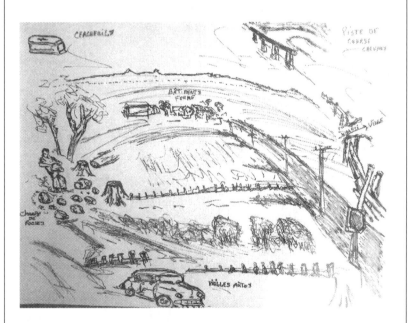

Figure 4.1 **The farm from my childhood and the neighbors.** Felt pencils, 46 cm × 61 cm (18″ × 24″).

I go back there in dreams, it may indicate that my current situation at the time of the dream does not meet a deep need for contact with friends and social stimulation.

It goes without saying that such dreams about exploring the boundaries of the farm are only one of the many themes of returning to childhood places. I also have many dreams where I go back to either rooms in the house or to various areas in the barn. There again, I see a familiar place and I enjoy being there, then I discover something new, new places or new arrays of objects. Questioning why I go back to a place rather than another, and what new objects refer to, provide information on the needs or feelings present in my life at some point.

I made a map of the farm and our neighboring boundaries (see Figure 4.1).

Portrait Gallery

We all have within us a whole lot of characters who more or less have a life of their own in our unconscious. They come from what Jungian analysts call *complexes* and *sub-personalities* (Jung, 2001). Most often and without us being aware of it, they influence our moods, our emotions, our spirit, our moments of depression and misery, as much as our feelings of well-being. Robert Johnson (1986) says, for example, that a man will only be happy if he has a positive relationship with the female figures from his dreams. These dreamlike characters spontaneously arise in our dreams in more or less variable forms: they may change forms. It proves helpful to learn how to identify them based on their typical energy in many of our dreams. Once an inner character has been identified, it becomes possible to integrate it into our portrait gallery by using drawing, painting, collage or sculpture. This way of getting in touch with our inner characters is particularly powerful: let's imagine our house or art studio filled with portraits of our sub-personalities! That is a very effective way of working to integrate all parts of us into a more coherent whole.

Once the characters of our portrait gallery have been created through drawing, painting, sculpture or collage, there are three ways to do work using them: *visual observation*, initiating an *active imagination dialogue* and *following the felt sense*. Any of those approaches can be used to explore and further our in-depth understanding of how these characters impact our whole life. Even when they appeared first in past dreams, it is likely that they are still part of us.

Visual Observation

Drawing, painting, sculpting or making a collage of a dream figure reveals details about the image and the character that we would not necessarily have noticed when writing down the dream, and these unexpected cues sometimes are all that is needed to understand who the character is to us. Taking the time to pay attention to every aspect of the character can add to our understanding of its impact on our inner life. The way the artistic production was done, over which we do not have full control, can be rich in messages about the significance of a character in our life. In short, it is a matter of taking the time to stay with the image, to use Shaun McNiff's wording (1992), in order to look closely at it and to let oneself be amazed by unexpected significance. We can also complete our visual observation of a character using the active imagination spoken dialogue.

Active Imagination Dialogue

This is about furthering the dream in the imagination by having a real conversation with the dream character. Even if the dialogue is imaginary, the interaction is significant and is marked by a real impact on the dreamer. It requires listening to what the character is telling us and being genuinely willing to get to know her or him. The difference with the Jungian dialogue approach (see Introduction in Chapter 2) where the questions that concern us are asked to a dream character, is that with active imagination, we exert much less control over the dialogue; the questions arise out of the emerging images and the actions of the character, as the dream is freely furthered through a dialogue.

However, the dialogue is "active" since we have to be actively involved in the exchange. We do this by sharing our agreements, unwillingness, objections, fears or any other reactions that arise while the dialogue unfolds on its own. If we're surprised at what we hear, it's a good indication that this active imagination is real. The purpose is to reach an understanding of how the character contributes to our psychic totality, but also to negotiate its place in our life and our choices.

The character may make requests, express its needs and request behavior changes or changes in values. It is imperative that we do not give in if our conscious "I" has doubts about the character's requests: our whole being must be in agreement with the requests or compromises reached through negotiation by both parties. It is rare indeed that it is only a matter of recognizing the existence of an inner character for harmony to be established. After all, if these parts of us are unconscious, having been denied the right to exist until now, negotiation is very likely to be necessary. The reasons for such a rejection are numerous and sometimes very important. They generally relate to some cultural objection from either the family environment or the school or social environment in which we have lived.

Becoming a more conscious and whole person implies acknowledging all these conditionings and making individual and personalized choices with regard to these more or less consciously imposed and adopted standards. This is what Jung meant by the word "individuation". So this whole process does not mean that we should accept the requests of our inner characters without any objection, as explained by Johnson (1986).

Following the Felt Sense

Using the felt sense to better understand an inner character requires that we identify ourselves with it, and then draw or paint our bodily feeling when picturing ourselves as being this character. Based on a purely physical sensation and likely abstract at first, this bodily feeling can deliver a lot of information about this part of ourselves. The feeling thus perceived will be more readily identified through its visual representation and will reveal unexpected aspects of ourselves, of an unknown potential, of an experience hitherto overlooked.

Power Animals

It can be quite surprising and very enlightening to browse through our dream journals in order to draw up a list of all animals appearing in our dreams. We usually don't pay attention to them unless they play a special role, for example in a nightmare. They often represent an instinctive part of us, that shows up to point out a tacit knowledge,[1] some wisdom that can help us in a life situation. When we are browsing through our dream journals, let us notice if a specific animal comes up repeatedly in relation to a given problem; there is a lot to be learned from examining the specifics of this animal: its surroundings, its unique attributes, its distinctive features, its social environment, etc.

Dream animals have a lot in common with the totem animals which are found in several Native American traditions in South and Central America (Villoldo, 2006a). According to these traditions, animal spirits can show up in our lives to help us grow and ensure our journey is as harmonious as possible. These guiding spirits often reveal themselves to us through synchronicity[2] and in our dreams.

We can paint an animal from our dream, make a mask of it or create a three-dimensional piece, then use one of the three typical methods to put the inner experience into words (see Introduction in Chapter 2), given that when an animal frequently occurs in our dream journals, it is wise to work on that dream figure to explore what existential message is carried.

Application Example

The following dream is a fascinating one from Françoise Pelletier, an art therapist from Québec, Canada who participated in a workshop on art therapy and Greek goddesses. It is a dream in which I myself play a role.

Jaguar Woman

I am in a southern town, and I am looking down from the tops of houses. The children are throwing balls. Then I go down and someone points out that there is a wild hare/ram coming out of the woods.

Then a jaguar is walking up to me, cool and very beautiful. I feel a little bit afraid, but everybody keeps calm and someone even says it is not dangerous and there is no need to worry.

The jaguar is moving forward, then Johanne sits down next to it and they start talking together using feline growls; they understand one another very well, but I do not understand the jaguar. I am reaching out to the jaguar, it offers me his paw, then I start understanding what it says. It has turned into an old lady dressed in a jaguar skin.

It is a very powerful scene that feels alive when I think back on it.

Françoise's Comments

Françoise then made a mask of this jaguar woman (see Figure 4.2). Here is what she said about it.

Inside the ears of the jaguar woman mask, I insert a pink shell and a mauve one, in order for me to always hear the sea, and to hear with my jaguar woman's ears what my unconscious is telling me.

Figure 4.2 ***The jaguar woman mask.*** Plaster cloth, acrylic, feathers, shells, etc. 23 cm × 15 cm (9¼″ × 6″).

I really like the mask and I find it very beautiful. I admire its feline look which tells me about the importance, in my life, of belonging to the clan of Artemis, the clan of the wild woman. I realize that I have Paule Lebrun's book, La Déesse et la panthère (2015) (The Goddess and the panther) at home; perhaps it will help me continue to do so. Moreover, I want to keep the mask at my bedside, so that it talks to me in my dreams.

MY OWN STRANGE EXPERIENCE REGARDING FRANÇOISE'S DREAM

While Françoise was telling her dream from the previous night during the Greek goddesses' session I was facilitating, I had a strange experience. Listening to her, tears started to stream down from my eyes but I could not understand why!

Realizing that this dream impacted me in some way since I was part of it, but above all because I reacted so very strongly and inexplicably, I made the decision to work on Françoise's dream as if it were mine. This is why I consider this experience to be one of the strangest I ever had, since, a priori, a dream can only belong to the dreamer herself.

Doing dreamwork using the active imagination approach, through re-entry into HER dream, I initiated a dialogue with the jaguar. I realized that it was as if Lillian, my art therapy teacher, with whom I had no longer any contact, but who had been an extremely significant person to me, was back to talk to me and that, if we had not understood each other for years, that was no longer the case because I finally understood her language. It felt like I was resolving a past conflict with her. This experience was both strange and calming.

Later, I learned that for Central American shamans, the jaguar is often seen as an animal spirit, and we were doing this workshop in Costa Rica. For the Laika people (Villoldo, 2006a), the jaguar represents the second step in the healing and growth process. As an animal, he is the guardian of the tropical forest; he has no predator other than humans and he is fearless. According to Alberto Villoldo, Ph. D., psychologist and medical anthropologist (2018, 2007, 2006a, 2000), the jaguar can guide us to explore the darkest places we fear within us, for us to find beauty. The jaguar primarily embodies the power to transform beliefs, ideas and emotions; it helps us understand that life crises are opportunities to die to something and to be reborn to something else. This is very close to the personal work that dreaming leads us to do.

Many South American shamans and some indigenous peoples strongly identify with the jaguar. Villoldo states that "the ability to communicate without words is one of the legendary attributes of Jaguar-Shamans" (2006a, p. 166). The connection with this dream is so surprising that I can only accept that many aspects of reality are lost to us, and it is in our best interest to open up to our inner world and to the dream realm, which are gateways to those uncommon realities of consciousness (Tart, 1990, 1986). The jaguar has remained a very important animal spirit for me, one that sometimes joins me for re-entry into my dreams. I found a very powerful image of a jaguar that assists me in my dialogues with it as a spirit animal. So can you with your own dream animal spirits.

Inner Child and Inner Adolescent

As with dream animals, we can browse our dream journals to determine whether children or adolescents are found in our dreams. Of course, they represent parts of ourselves, whether it be our own inner child or inner adolescent, or what our relationship with children or teenagers close to us feels like. How do those children or adolescents feel in our dreams? Are they happy? Are they sad? Are they sick? Have they passed away? What are they doing? What are they dressed like? What is their relationship with other children or teenagers? With adults? The answers to these questions do not have to be taken literally, but rather should be taken as symbols, by questioning what those dreams meant at the time when we had them. It is possible to witness how our inner child has evolved in our psyche over time. It can grow from early childhood to adolescence, if we have taken care of him through dreamwork or otherwise. A previous childhood or adolescence dream can also be worked on as though we were dreaming about it now, and we may try to identify the message from it.

Jung (1991) talks about the child archetype. It is comprised of several components, including the wounded child and the creative child. While the creative child holds treasures of vitality and creativity, we nevertheless need to have access to his resources. To do that, we often have to start by taking care of our wounded child. Whitfield (2016), Bradshaw (1992a), Capaccione (1991), Taylor (1992), Whitfield et Nuckols (1987) and specifically Alice Miller (2008a, 2004, 1990, 1987, 1986, 1983) are all authors who have written on the matter and can help us know how to take care of the wounded child.

In our dream journals, it is possible therefore to witness the condition of our inner child, how he was affected by the happy or unfortunate events of our lives, to see if he has grown up, to witness the evolution or the deterioration in his well-being . . . Our inner adolescent has also gone through lots of experiences that may have had decisive impacts on the paths that we chose and our well-being in adulthood.

Application Example

The Adolescent

I am dreaming that I am a teenager sitting on a rock. She is looking directly at me with seriousness and without shame.

Dreamer's Comments

I decided to initiate a Jungian dialogue with her. What I understood from this is that my inner adolescent has grown up and become stronger. I'm glad to see how well, comfortable and confident she looks. It was certainly not the case at the time I was a teenager!

Inner Artist

Whether we are an artist or are simply interested in arts, or even if we think we have no artistic talent at all, it is very possible that the artist within us has deployed its creativity in our dreams. His or her style, colors, stories, preferences and harmonics will become apparent by exploring its presence in our dream journals over time. We can read our dreams again and take note of any discrete paintings hung on the walls of our dream homes, any music pieces played by one of the dream's characters, a performing dancer, a novel getting written night after night or even an artist making a painting. It may be difficult to reproduce the painting or the music piece from a past dream if we failed to note the details of our art creation, but we can somehow draw inspiration from it to initiate artistic work.

A conference on dreams is hosted annually by the International Association for the Study of Dreams (IASD)[3] in the United States or Europe. The event includes a showcase featuring visual artworks inspired from dreams. As for me, I identified three ways in which we can develop visual artwork from dreams.

First Way: Painting a Part of a Dream

We can simply choose an object, an animal, a character or a dreamscape and reproduce it as closely as possible. Dreams are filled with inspiring themes and the dreamlike dimension, which feels somewhat strange, makes them all the more interesting.

Second Way: Drawing Inspiration from the Lines, Forms and Colors in a Dream

Without choosing to specifically represent an object, an animal, a character or a specific dreamscape, the fact remains that finding inspiration in the lines, shapes, colors, movements, atmospheres or themes from a dream can give birth to uniquely styled artwork. The surrealist painters painted in this way, reproducing the dreamlike atmosphere of dreams. Dali's paintings representing timepieces such as *The Persistence of Memory* or *Melting Watch* are two famous examples, as well as *The Sacrament of the Last Supper*, based on a different theme.

Third Way: Reproducing a Dream's Emotional Energy

Jill Mellick (2001) refers to this unique painting process when she suggests reproducing the energy of a dream. She suggests taking time to feel a dream in our body, then letting this energy pass from our arm and hand into a pencil on paper. Kim Vergil, an artist from Montreal who now lives in Switzerland, partly draws inspiration from this painting process. She uses a mixed-media technique consisting of photographs and acrylic paint. Here is what she says about her artwork: "My creative process is inspired by how I understand we create our night dreams. Dreams are a combination of images stitched together and interwoven with our emotional energy. My mixed media approach is a combination of personal collaged photographs on canvas plus an energetic application of paint as the emotional energy that ties it all together" (www.artsyshark.com/2017/08/08/featured-artist-kim-vergil/).[4]

Dream Mantis and Dream Shield

Just like for the making of an actual *Dream Shield*, a *Dream Mantis* involves representing a set of past and current dreams on a three-dimensional support such as a piece of leather or fabric. The dreams may be picked for their common similarities, just like for a series of dreams, or out of an intuitive sense that they have to be used in combination. Each selected dream is represented on the leather or fabric support using acrylic paint for one of its features (character, object, animal, dreamscape), or else one of the dream's objects is created then attached to the support. When completed, this artwork usually takes on an unforeseen meaning: it summarizes parts of our experience in a nuanced way and provides us with solutions for our well-being. It immediately becomes a valuable and meaningful piece that will continue to take on even greater meaning many years after its creation. At least this is what people who did it have experienced. All the people I saw making such objects noticed how they were consistently meaningful, creative and how they turned out to be unique treasures.

Application Example

Francine's Dream Mantis

During a five-day intensive session on dreams where participants were invited to make a *Dream Shield*, Francine's turned out to be instead a *Dream Mantis*. Francine made it her shamanic mantis, a symbol of her personal power. Twenty-one years later, it still features in her arts studio and remains meaningful for her (see Figure 4.3). Here is how she describes her dreamwork process:

At first, I cut out a butterfly shape from a piece of fabric. This basic shape was to serve as a support to which symbols featuring different dreams would be attached throughout the week.

This butterfly then turned into a Dream Mantis, from my very first dream. During the night, I heard a voice inviting me to head north. The next morning, I went walking, heading northbound through the woods around the Orford Arts Centre, using the compass I had borrowed. I found a

Figure 4.3 **The dream mantis.** Fabric, leather in various colors, fur, wool, pearls, buttons, 1.32 m × 1.37 m (4′4″ × 4′6″) when fully extended.

*dead butterfly (symbolizing my illusions) along the way and I buried it.
When I got back to the arts studio, I picked a fur collar and I sew it onto
the upper part of the butterfly-shaped fabric, to represent my northern
dream. That is how the butterfly turned into a Mantis . . .*

The following is another dream I had during the workshop.

Needing to See

*I am in an antique shop. I am looking around. I am looking for some-
thing but I do not know what. Two teenagers are also in the shop. They
are laughing and having fun. I suddenly realize that I can't see clearly
because I do not have my glasses. I do not understand how I could possibly have forgotten. I feel uncomfortable without my glasses. I have a
blurry vision.*

*On my Mantis, I put two buttons representing two clear and transpar-
ent eyes serving to harbor my intention to develop a clear vision.*

*These are the only two other dreams I had during the workshop week. I had
the other dreams that served to create my Dream Mantis before the workshop.
Here is one of these past dreams:*

This Tree is My Ally

*I am going to see my mother who lives on the second floor. I know my
sister is there. Instead of going through the front door, I climb into the
tree which is in front of the house. When I reach the balcony, I leave the
two books that I brought with me on a large branch (in its Y-shaped hollow), thinking to myself that I must not forget them on my way out. The
balcony is old and damaged. I move very slowly and cautiously, but the
floor gives way and my leg falls through. I then ask my mother who is
inside the house to go find my sister so that she can come and help me.
I got out of that bad situation with the help of my sister using a chair, but
I can't figure out how.*

*To represent that dream on my Dream Mantis, I cut out a big tree
shape into a piece of brown leather and I sew it with red wool. The tree
alone takes up almost half of the space. By its size, this tree becomes
the main symbol stating my intention to connect with nature. The walk
in the wilderness (from my first dream) invites me to make contact with
the plant world. This tree alone represents a force of nature, a life
force: imposing and strong, with a rooting equal to its great presence
which makes it almost invincible. I identify with this tree that stands
on solid ground between heaven and earth. In my very soul, I yearn to*

become a strong, dependable and responsible person who serves her community.

When I climb the tree, I can feel its strength and I feel connected to it, which allows me to act like a child, that is climbing a tree rather than going up the stairs, as adults would do. By climbing the tree, I am invited to reconnect with my inner child and to have fun while providing the effort necessary to get stronger and become, in my eyes, a force of nature (rather than a victim). Like the tree, I want to be firmly rooted into the earth and expand into space, seeking balance and harmony.

Existential Message from the Dream about the Tree

Accept this call to climb the tree as an invitation to reconnect with your soul and your inner child. Learn how to better put down roots in order to better move on up.

The Mantis

I've been cleaning up my arts studio lately, and I gave or threw away a lot of things, but I couldn't get rid of the Mantis/Shield I created 21 years ago. It seems to me that it was only yesterday. I feel nostalgic about the disposing of a symbol reflecting a deep, sincere and intense week-long investment. But I think there is something even more important than that, in other words the feeling that I had gone right to the very core of myself in this Dream Mantis.

By doing research to offer my small contribution to this book, I realize that the Mantis/Shield alone carries all the wishes of my soul regarding my life on earth. The spiral image clearly represents the idea that all of the unconscious aspirations and desires of my soul were present before and continued to evolve and develop.

How it Relates with My Own Story and My Reality

As a teenager, I took residential school painting classes at boarding school. At that time, I secretly cherished the dream of becoming an artist. I was very pleased to study Fine Arts, and when I made my first solo exhibition long after my studies, I understood that there was a greater happiness than that of painting, namely seeing the guests react with excitement at my opening by taking ownership of what I had projected onto the canvases. They were all applying their personal interpretation by seeing themselves through images. Then I secretly started cherishing the dream of becoming an art therapist. I became an art therapist because of my great happiness and delight in help-ing the people I accompanied on their journey to grow bigger and stronger through their ability to project outwardly their most intimate inner self. Daring to be, daring to become visible, daring to create and daring to create oneself.

When I attended the workshop about Dreams, Art Therapy and Healing, where I created my Dream Mantis/Shield, I cherished even more secretly my dream of becoming a shaman. The dance between night-dreams and reality and between the conscious and the unconscious that I created, practiced and explored throughout the week was fascinating and exciting and I identified with it deeply inside of me. Following the workshop, I cherished my dream of becoming a shaman in many ways: dream circles, talking circles, sweat lodges, vision quests, paying attention to the wounded healer, rituals, rites of passage and Medicine Wheels from different traditions. Finally, I learned to give energy treatments, like polarity therapy and shamanic healing based on the five elements.

My Dream Mantis/Shield reminds me of the path travelled to get close to who I am. I am not an artist, not a shaman, but a woman who has overcome many fears, including the fear of death. A woman who is fully human and has more compassion and more love to share. A woman with faith: faith in mankind and in the invisible. This Dream Mantis/Shield reminds me every moment that I can live in full harmony with myself, with other people and with nature by accepting to be who I am simply and humbly.

Francine Duguay, Art Therapist, Sherbrooke, Québec, Canada.

Dream Series Fairy Tale

A story written from a series of dreams is developed after identifying dreams that we feel speak to the same theme, especially a life transition moment. As explained for the method called *storytelling* (see Chapter 2), everything is necessarily dramatized in a story; kings, queens, dragons and witches, as well as extreme hardships and magic are brought into play. At first, it is easier to let the story develop spontaneously, just as it comes to you, and subsequently to refine it, up to that point where it totally suits you. You will then see what new knowledge the story brings about yourself.

Personally, I decided to write a story about my transition to retirement, considering that I had noted 14 dreams that spoke to my experience about it, over the span of two years before retiring and seven months after. It would be too long to expose all of them here, but I will provide excerpts of five typical dreams about my journey, that I had before, upon and after my retirement from the university where I was teaching art therapy full time.

Application Example

MY DREAMS REFLECTING THE TRANSITION TO RETIREMENT

DREAM #1 – 20 MONTHS BEFORE RETIREMENT, I FELT BURNED OUT AND THIS
DREAM REFLECTED IT.

A Swimming Lesson in Ice Cold Water

I have a swimming lesson in a pool filled with ice cold water and large chunks of ice. The teacher is asking us to do an exercise in the deep end of the swimming pool and to even go beneath the ice. I am afraid of this. The other students do not feel secure either. So, I say to the teacher "I am leaving this class. I don't even have to be here and I don't take pleasure in this class."

I woke up happy about the choice I had made during the dream of not forcing myself to do something that didn't make sense to me. The existential message was that I could choose an early retirement if I wanted to.

At that time, 20 months before retirement, I also had a dream called RISK OF FLOODING that was related in Chapter 1 to explain the Haïku method. I had understood that I was feeling very sad because it felt as though I was leaving people behind, despite the fact that the boat had become much too heavy!

DREAM #2 – THREE MONTHS BEFORE RETIREMENT.

The Small White House

I have to take a boat to go somewhere with my partner. To get to the boat, I must first enter a small white house with yellow wood embellishments, that is located on the waterfront. The steps leading to the front door form a small and narrow dark blue staircase. When I go up the stairs, the steps move or oscillate and I risk falling. For his part, my partner does not climb the stairs. He goes to the right side of the house, where a small door sheltered by a roof and surrounded by light wood walls on each side leads to the ground surface without the need to step up to enter the house. I am really surprised and I wonder why I should go up the staircase, and he is not. I am jealous!

The existential message from the dream was that I too could enjoy retirement in simplicity, like my partner who enjoys it! No need to create fear and misery in advance!

DREAM #3 – TWO MONTHS BEFORE RETIREMENT, AT A TIME WHEN ALL THAT REMAINED TO DO FOR ME WAS TO CLOSE THE FILES.

I Am Off-Loading from the Plane!

I am onboard a Big 747 aircraft. It stopped to let me get off. I am standing in front of the open door from the plane side. I'm opening a very large document. It actually looks like a folder containing important diplomas. I open the folder and find three sheets stating that it is a success. There is no staircase to step down the plane, but on the ground, there are many people waiting for me and encouraging me. They are saying I will get help. I end up on the ground. I have a sense of joy and lightness.

I found it quite surprising to have such a clear dream that is so closely related to my inner experience. The existential message is that I successfully did the work that had to be done, that it is now over and that I will not be alone for the next phase of my life. I make a connection with the number three and the three art therapy programs I helped develop at the university.

DREAM #4 – TWO MONTHS AFTER RETIREMENT.

Cleaning up the Basement of My Friend's House

I am dreaming that my close friend Michelle is cleaning out her papers. As I go down to the basement of her house, I see that it is completely empty and I am very impressed with it. There is absolutely nothing left, just a few paper sheets here and there, no more than two or three. Then it's time to leave; my friend and I both burst into tears. I say to her "You helped me live", and she answers that I helped her live too. I really feel very moved.

Reflecting on this dream about cleaning out papers, I understand that it is about grieving for my twenty-year-old job. The existential message is that this relationship with the university is over, that it has helped me grow and that I, too, have helped it grow, which is the truth.

DREAM #5 – SIX MONTHS AFTER RETIREMENT.

The Large Golden Canvas

I am sitting in a room where a group is doing artwork. On a long rectangular-shaped table, I am creating a painting on a very long and large paper sheet using golden paint. The golden color reminds me of the Buddhist Temples I visited a short time ago.

Many persons who sit next to each other are also painting at other tables. These persons are former college and university coworkers. I am looking at them, all sitting together while I am alone, painting at my table. In my dream, it seems to me that I am somewhere else, apart from them, and that I do not belong to the group anymore, with a twinge of regret. But I also feel that I do accept this and that I have feelings of tenderness for them.

There is a man who is doing a painting on a large golden canvas on the wall. He is a former colleague, but I do not know exactly who. Then he moves away from it, and every time he is shaking a small puppet, a frightening little character suddenly appears on the canvas, with its hair standing on end and its teeth out. It looks floodlit through the canvas.

Then I notice that while he draws our attention with his puppet, another guy is projecting a light on the canvas that causes the little character to come up, who was incorporated into the canvas using invisible paint.

In this dream, I understand that I am integrating and accepting retirement more and more, despite fears that come up from time to time, such as the possibility of disease and death that come with older age.

The Fairy Tale: The Princess in Exile (inspired by the five preceding dreams)

Once upon a time, there was a princess who lived in a large castle with fine stones and solid foundations. She was happy. One day, though, she felt that something was not right anymore and that she had to leave to find her own kingdom. Would she have to face dragons, flooding, dangers of all kinds when traveling through unknown lands? And to where? She felt very sad to leave her friends behind, she feared that she would get lost along the way, feel worthless and no longer be recognized, in countries where she was never heard of.

When the time came, she felt ready to face the journey through all dangers. That day, a good fairy came to her and advised her to travel a different, much simpler road, assuring her that it would be a much safer path. So, she left a little more lighthearted.

At the end of a long journey where she met neither dragons nor highwaymen, she suddenly ended up at another castle where she was welcomed with open arms. She was given many presents and a large parchment proclaiming that she was now the queen of that land.

After a few months of her new life, she realized with astonishment that she had almost stopped thinking of her former life, that she accepted more and more her loss, and that if demons appeared at times on the walls of her new castle, she was well aware that it was just her own fears playing tricks on her.

Dreamer's Comments: What I Got from that Story

Selecting the dreams about retirement from my journals and telling my personal story gave me a sense of where I was at this time of transition and helped me see that despite my fears and miseries, the journey went smoothly. A new life began with its own unique challenges. After all, one does not retire without realizing that almost a lifetime has passed and that we have fewer years ahead of us than before. But I still have to achieve my painting on the large golden canvas, and I keep on writing, painting, teaching and practicing art therapy in that new land, where false fears are sometimes created.

Treasure Boxes

Our dreams hold a wealth of treasures! Fascinating, timeless and universal symbols, mysterious objects, mythical animals . . . It can be very meaningful to read our dreams again with the goal of bringing out all the symbols that might even have gone unnoticed at the time. From these, we can make amulets or decks of symbols.

The Amulets Box

An *amulets box* contains a set of stones about the same size, on which the symbols brought out from our dreams will be painted with acrylic paint. The painted stones will then be coated with a medium, like a plastic varnish, to make them waterproof. Then the stones can serve as a tarot deck for reference as needed, using it the same way as traditional tarot cards. No need to try reproducing the typical Arcana and characters from tarot decks: it is your own personal divination set.

As for tarot cards, we formulate a question for something we want to clarify, and then we randomly pick one stone or even several ones for the same question; for example, regarding *"before, during, after"* an issue, or else we can do what is often done with tarot decks: ask questions like *"what works in favor of, what works against, what are the outcomes . . . "*, or any combination desired.

It is helpful to jot down from which dream(s) each symbol painted on a stone was brought out, what was the context of the dream(s), as well as the meaning associated to the symbols in each relevant dream. If ever re-reading such information does not help you understand the message carried by a symbol upon drawing a stone, just use the opportunity to look it up in a dictionary of symbols,[5] or to initiate a Jungian dialogue with it (see Introduction, Chapter 2).

Card Decks

Instead of painting symbols from dreams on stones, we can make drawings or paintings on cards of a standard size decided beforehand. Similarly, these cards may also be used as a personal tarot deck. The dream(s) where a symbol appeared may be noted on the back of each card, as well as the relevant context of the dream(s) and what it meant for us at the time we had this/these dream(s).

The Box Itself

You can choose a treasure box that looks attractive to you for your amulets or cards, and decorate it to your taste using paint, drawings, glued pictures, fabric, etc.

Personal Spiritual Altar

Many peoples and spiritual or religious traditions have a ritual practice of creating a small altar at home that is dedicated to spiritual beings, gods, goddesses or ancestors. With a lifetime of dream journals, such characters are likely to be found in our dream stories. As an example, we can create a small personal spiritual altar on a base made of silk fabric, leather skin or a piece of fabric we like or else on a ceremonial mat or in a sandtray box. Miniatures, small statuettes or paper-craft representations may be used and glued on paperboard to make them stand upright. This is only one of several options, and it is up to us to use our imagination to invent our own altar.

Essentially, the above-mentioned characters are representations of what Jung called the *Self*, the sacred part of us (Von Franz, 2008, 2006, 1992). We may initiate a dialogue with these characters when we need to connect with our own wisdom in a complex situation. On the altar, we can also arrange personal guides, spirit animals and possibly ancestors who are dear to us, that emerged in our dreams to help us out. It is important that they be wise and positive figures from our spiritual life. It is not about praying to them, but rather to have visual symbols at hand to help us connect with our spiritual life and our inner wisdom.

Figure 4.4 ***My personal spiritual altar.*** Figurines in a sandtray box, 75 cm × 50 cm × 7 cm
(30″ × 20″ × 3″).

Application Example

Going through my dream journals, I have noticed several interesting spiritual characters. In addition, I remembered that I had a dream about the Egyptian goddess Nefertiti a long time ago. I also had dreams about the Greek goddesses Aphrodite and Athena, as well as the Egyptian cat goddess Bast, and most recently, Buddha, after a trip to Thailand. I also know I have had many dreams about Virgin Mary and Saint Anne, her mother. I love that the spiritual characters from my dreams are a mix of many past and current religious and spiritual traditions. Each of them has something different to teach me, and according to what my intuition tells me, I pick one or the other to initiate a dialogue with or even several of them, to find answers to some of my questions. At times, their mere presence on the altar reminds me of important principles. For example, I know that the Egyptian goddess Bast reminds me to dare to express how I feel deep down inside (see Mask Making, Chapter 2).

Personal Dream Dictionary

Having a large number of dreams whose existential messages have been elucidated makes it possible to see that certain symbols are recurring and have similar meanings from one dream to another. Taking note of them will allow you to develop some kind of personal dictionary of dreams. In this way, we will have references available to elucidate the messages of our future dreams, taking care however to never take anything for granted. A single symbol can have a totally different meaning to the same person in a different living situation.

Thus, I have become aware over time that boats, especially large cruise ships, foretell new and significant awareness regarding my psychological life, and ever since then I took every opportunity to work on dreams about cruise ships. Dreams about cars teach me how I lead my life in certain situations: going too fast, driving a car with bad breaks . . . letting someone else drive my car . . . Flooding tells me of deep sorrow or loss. Dreams where everything suddenly turns black indicate a serious illness or some-one's death.

These meanings do not necessarily apply to someone else's dreams: you just have to see for yourself with your dreamwork. It is a fact that you may be better off with figuring out the personal meaning of a specific symbol for yourself, since dictionaries of dreams can be misleading. And that is the point of building up a personal dream dictionary.

Life Overview

Many dreamers write their dreams for 10, 20, 30 years . . . 50 years and even more! Bringing out the issues present in our dreams at 20, 30 or 40 years can prove to be very interesting, since our life experiences and challenges are different from one decade to the next.

For this, we can draw inspiration from Erik Erickson's (1982/1959) theory, stating eight major psychosocial crises associated with eight stages of life. Overall, for Erikson, human development involves shifting from a state of *non-self identity* to a state of *self-identity* (Thomas & Michel, 1994); which means going through a process allowing us to gain greater self-knowledge about who we are. The challenges to face at each stage of life for a healthy psychological development are identified. Each age is described in terms of contrast between two personality traits and each individual is somewhere on a continuum between the two opposites (Thomas & Michel, 1994). The challenges associated with each stage span the entire lifetime. They are described below from Erikson's perspective. Specific issues that affected your inner child or inner adolescent, as well as issues affecting your adult life, can be identified in your dreams.

According to Erikson, the Eight Stages of Life are the following:

AGE 0 TO 1: TRUST OR BASIC MISTRUST

Depending on whether the basic needs of a child are reasonably met in the first year of life, the child will develop a sense of trust in the world around him or, on the contrary, a basic mistrust. Trust is defined as "the act of being able to predict and depend on one's own behaviour and that of others" (Thomas & Michel, 1994, p. 19 of the electronic version of the chapter about Erikson).

AGE 1 TO 3: AUTONOMY OR SHAME AND DOUBT

This stage is linked to the anal stage according to Freud, where the main challenge is the sphincter control. Many issues take place at this stage. Children learn how to control bowel movements and develop a sense of power when successful, which is the basis for a sense of autonomy. This is the *Terrible Two* stage where the child, with his sense of power, is trying to control everything, including his parents. Depending on whether or not parents are able to set clear limits and to remain flexible and patient regarding the learning of sphincter control at their child's own pace, children will be able to develop an autonomous personality or, on the contrary, will become obsessive and stuck with shame and doubt, if toilet training is too rigid, for example.

AGE 3 TO 6: INITIATIVE OR GUILT

Children take more and more initiatives in games serving to explore their role in the world and their social identity. They want to be considered as unique and need positive attention, otherwise they may develop guilt and anxiety for being who they are. Guilt can be associated with sexual impulses, since this is the age of Oedipus conflict. For this conflict to be properly resolved, children must receive from the same-sex parent responses approving their interest in sexuality, and from the opposite-sex parent, responses that they are attractive but need to find a partner their age.

FROM AGE 6 TO ADOLESCENCE: INDUSTRY OR INFERIORITY

When entering elementary school, children need to affirm their personal worth by doing schoolwork that proves meaningful. They may develop a sense of powerlessness and inferiority if they are ill-prepared to enter school or if the tasks assigned are too difficult or not rightly valued by their environment (Thomas & Michel, 1994).

AGE 12 TO 18: IDENTITY OR ROLE CONFUSION DURING ADOLESCENCE

In search for an identity, adolescents experience some confusion for a long time. Puberty and a fast-changing body as well as changes in social roles and expectations about them create a deep confusion in adolescents. For Erikson, the major challenge for adolescents at this age is that they need to confirm that their own way of being is acceptable for the society they live in.

Erikson (1982/1959) also distinguishes life stages in adulthood:

AGE 20–30 (APPROXIMATELY): INTIMACY AND SOLIDARITY OR ISOLATION

If young adults emerge from adolescence with a reasonable sense of their own identity, then they will be able to establish sexual and intellectual intimacy with a partner and reach compromises with others. That requires feeling secure enough with one's identity to be able to stand for it against anything that could threaten the integrity of the Self. It is a time for setting values about one's relationships and working life.

AGE 30–50 (APPROXIMATELY): PRODUCTIVITY OR STAGNATION

Reaching a mature age, adults feel the need to pass on something, either to a future generation by building a family, or by wanting to contribute to something worthwhile for society. Creating and generating ideas is important at that age. If the need to pass on something is not met, there is a sense of stagnation.

OVER 50 YEARS (ACCORDING TO OTHER SOURCES: OVER 65 YEARS): INTEGRITY OR DESPAIR

The most important question for persons of that age is if they feel they have lived a full life, if they have accepted their own lifestyle or not and can even defend the dignity of their choices, of their particular lifestyle in spite of eventual difficulties (Erikson, 1994, cited in Thomas & Mitchel, 1994). Whenever conflicts or life stages failed to be resolved, the individual can feel despair.

Yolanda Jacobi (1983), a Jungian author, states that a major crisis occurs in mid-life. According to her, the two ages of life are youth, where the challenge is to find your place in the world and how you can contribute to the community, and the second half of life, where the *spiritual self* becomes the focus of the psyche. One day, the individual becomes aware of the inevitability of aging and death, and then values and priorities change, for both men and women. Jung (1993) says it is necessary that a psychotherapy analysis be conducted differently based on each age of life.

There are other writers who can shed light on life issues that may emerge from our dreams. See among others Dechavanne et Tavoillot (2008); Singer (1990); Houde (1986); and Gail Sheehy (1997, 2006, 1982, 1977) in particular, who has written a lot about life stages and whose books are still relevant.

With these stages in mind, reading through our dream journals can help identify how we personally experienced these life stages. Maybe we will find that these stages do not apply per se to our life. The most important is that this exercise provides us with a kind of life review, which might prove to be essential at times for guiding our life choices. As an example, it is often said that the fifties are the decade of last chance, when it is still possible to begin fulfilling meaningful dreams. Jacobi (1983) reports that the transition from the first half to the second half of life often comes with very distressing crises, like divorce, changes in occupation or residence, financial losses, or physical or psychological illnesses of all kinds. These growth crisis phases come with or bring about the transition to the second half of life.

Reading through our dream journals can allow us to take stock of our life. In this way, our life review will be inclusive of the deep psychological realm of dreams.

Notes

1. According to Sela-Smith (2002): "The tacit dimension of personal knowledge is that internal place where experience, feeling and meaning join together to form both a picture of the world and a way to navigate that world. Tacit knowledge is a continually growing, multileveled, deep-structural organization that exists for the most part outside of ordinary awareness and is the foundation on which all other knowledge stands. This deep dimension of knowledge in under construction each time a new experience is introduced" (p. 60).
2. Synchronicity is defined as the occurrence of a meaningful coincidence that is too significant to be just a coincidence; it usually relates to our inner life. For example, a dreamer dreams about a lion and during the day, different people talk about lions, invite him to go see a documentary about lions, point out a picture of a lion in a magazine, etc.
3. See their website at www.iasd.com.
4. Please go to www.kimvergil.com for her artwork examples.
5. The most interesting dictionaries of symbols I found are: Chevalier, J., & Gheerbrant, A. (1982). *Dictionnaire des symboles*. Paris: Robert Laffont/Jupiter; Romey, G. (2005). *Dictionnaire de la symbolique des rêves*. Paris: Albin Michel and Rohnnberg, A., & Martin, K. (2011). *Le livre des symboles: Réflexions sur des images archétypales*. Köln: Taschen.

Conclusion

With the completion of this second book on dreams, I believe I voiced the most important points about creative and art therapy dreamwork methods and surveyed all existing art therapy methods. As always, remember that only the dreamer is capable of identifying the true meaning of their dreams. It is meaningful to me that I provided you with a variety of resources to find the messages of your dreams by yourself. I cannot stress enough how much it will help you feel empowered as you understand and master more and more of your inner life and develop happiness and joy because of this innermost work.

As I mentioned earlier, what you need to do now is try these creative and art therapy methods! Use them regularly and experiment with several of them. That's how you will be able to identify those that work best for you and those with which you have the most affinities. Observe their impact on your personal transformation: you most probably will gain inner peace and joy, and suffer less turmoil, agitation, anxiety or unpleasant emotions.

This book provides helpful information about nightmares. The different types and functions of nightmares will help you make sense of them and the five-steps method to work on them will help to dissipate them and ensure that they never return. This method emerged in the course of my art therapy practice through the years and through working on my own nightmares. I am indeed pleased with the results and I believe you will be too.

I invite you to pursue your personal creative and art therapy dreamwork. There is so much to learn about yourself, so many treasures to find in your psyche and so much self-reliance and well-being to gain through dreamwork. I can only hope that you see the value and interest of your own dreamwork and that you continue to keep dream journals your whole life.

Appendix
How to Remember Your Dreams[1]

The following methods can help you remember your dreams.

Set the alarm clock 15 to 20 minutes in advance to take time to recall the images and sensations upon waking. This is often effective enough to remember your dreams. Please avoid reviewing your daily schedule; you might want to stay in touch with the images and feelings present on waking, laying still in bed and keeping your eyes closed.

After holding still for a while, try another position you like to sleep in. As a matter of fact, it is easier to remember a dream by getting into the position you were sleeping in.

Keep a pencil and a notebook by the bed. When waking up, jot down a few key words about the images in your dream so that they can be brought back to your mind when you read them in the morning, given one often wakes up at night following a dream. You don't even need to turn on the light to write down these few words.

Upon waking, please take note right away of the dreams you remember since the images will quickly vanish. Dreams will return to your mind in reverse order: the last scene in the last dream, followed with the previous scene, then the second to last dream and so on.

Open your Dream Journal every morning, whether you had a dream or not. If you did not have any, please take note of the blurry sensations and emotions present upon waking up and make up a night dream. It will include unconscious cues as though it was an actual dream. In the face of the determination displayed, the unconscious will finally capitulate and you will have *actual* dream material.

Value all cues. At the end of the night, please note everything even if it's only a sound, an image or a sensation as if they were dreams, and your dreamwork will be profitable. The more you value your dreams and work with them, the more they return to your mind.

Use the incubation approach. While falling asleep, affirm repeatedly that you will remember your dreams upon waking up in the morning.

Initiate a dialogue about your resistance to remembering your dreams. You might ask questions like: "Why are you staying away from me?" and listen to the answers that will come from deep within. As for me, I once had the following answer "You have enough dream material to review for now, just work on the dreams you currently have". This answer was in fact consistent with my current reality. Once this dream material was finally elucidated, I was able to remember my dreams.

With all these tips, you will eventually come to remember your dreams successfully. Just be persistent.

Note

1. This tipsheet was first published in French in Hamel, J. (2017/1993). *Rêves, art-thérapie et guérison: De l'autre côté du miroir*. Montréal: Québec-Livres, and in English in Hamel, J. (2021). *Dreams, art therapy and healing: Beyond the looking glass*. New York: Routledge.

Bibliography

American Psychiatric Association. (2013). *Mini-desk reference to the diagnostic criteria from the DSM-V*. Washington, DC: APA.

Arnulf, L. (2016). Pourquoi rêvons-nous? *Pour la science*. January no. 459. Paris: Traduction of Scientific American.

Auel, J. M. (2014). *Les enfants de la terre* (Vol. 1). Paris: Presses de la Cité.

Barrett, D. (1992). Through a glass darkly: Images of the dead in dreams. *Omega*, *24*(2), 97–108.

Baylor, G. W. & Deslauriers, D. (1987). *Le rêve, sa nature, sa fonction et une méthode d'analyse*. Sillery: Université du Québec.

Boa, F. (1994). *The way of the dream: Conversations on Jungian dream interpretation with Marie-Louise von Franz*. Boston and London: Shambhala.

Bosnak, R. (1988). *A little course in dreams*. Boston, MA: Shambala.

Bradshaw, J. (1992a). *Homecoming: Reclaiming and healing your inner child*. New York: Bantam.

Bradshaw, J. (1992b). *Retrouver l'enfant en soi: partez à la découverte de votre enfant intérieur*. Montréal: Le Jour.

Bulkeley, K. (2000). *Transforming dreams: Learning spiritual lessons from the dreams you never forget*. New York: John Wiley and Sons.

Bulkeley, K. & Bulkeley, P. (2005). *Dreaming beyond death: A guide to pre-death dreams and visions*. Boston, MA: Beacon Press.

Cameron, J. (2010). *La source de la créativité: L'art de la persévérance*. Boisbriand: Éditions Octave.

Cameron, J. (1992). *The artist's way: A spiritual path to higher creativity*. New York: Tarcher/Putnam.

Campbell, J. (1989). *Historical atlas of world mythology: The way of the animal powers* (Vol. 1); *The way of the seeded earth* (Vol. II). New York: Harper and Row.

Campbell, J. (1988). *The power of myth*. New York: Doubleday.

Campbell, J. (1968). *The hero with a thousand faces*. Princeton, NJ: Princeton University Press.

Capaccione, L. (1991). *Recovery of your inner child: The highly acclaimed method for liberating your inner self*. New York: Simon and Schuster/Fireside.

Castaneda, C. (1974). *Journey to Ixtlan: The lessons of Don Juan*. New York: Washington Square Press.

Chevalier, J. & Gheerbrant, A. (1982). *Dictionnaire des symboles*. Paris: Robert Laffont/Jupiter.

Clerc, O. (1986). *Vivre ses rêves*. Québec: Guy Saint-Jean-Élios.

Collectif de l'arc-en-ciel. (1991). *Et si les rêves servaient à nous éveiller?* Montréal: Quebecor.

Corrière, R. & Hart, J. (1978). *Les Maîtres-Rêveurs: Réapprenez à vivre avec vos rêves et vos sentiments*. Montréal: Scriptomedia.

Covey, S. R. (2013). *The 7 habits of highly effective people: Powerful lessons in personal change*. New York: Simon and Schuster.

Davis, J. L. & Wright, D. C. (2007). Randomized clinical trial for treatment of chronic nightmares in trauma-exposed adults. *Journal of Traumatic Stress, 20*(2), 123–133.

Dechavanne, E. & Tavoillot, P.-H. (2008). *Philosophie des âges de la vie*. Paris: Hachette Pluriel.

Dee, N. (1989). *The Dreamer's workbook*. Wellingborough, England: Aquarian Press.

Delaney, G. (1996). *Living your Dreams. The Classic Bestseller on Becoming Your Own Dream Expert*. San Francisco: HarperSanFrancisco.

Desjarlais, R. R. (1991). Dreams, divination, and Yolmo ways of knowing. *Dreaming Journal of the Association for the Study of Dreams, 1*(3).

Duchastel, A. (2005). *La voie de l'imaginaire: le processus en art-thérapie*. Montréal: Quebecor.

Erikson, E. H. (2013). *Childhood and society*. New York and London: W. W. Norton and Company.

Erikson, E. H. (1998/1994). *Adolescence et crise: La quête de l'identité*. Paris: Flammarion.

Erikson, E. H. (1994). *Identity and the Life Cycle*. New York and London: WW Norton.

Erikson, E. H. (1982/1959). *Enfance et société* (7' ed.). Paris: Delachaux and Niestle.

Faraday, A. (1976). *The dream game*. New York: Harper and Row.

Faraday, A. (1973). *Dream power*. New York: Berkley Medallion Books.

Foreman, E. (1988). *Awakening: A dream journal*. New York: Tabori and Chang.

Freud, S. (2016/1900). *L'interprétation des rêves: Les fiches de lecture d'Universalis*. Éd. Kindle.

Frost, S. B. (2010). *SoulCollage evolving: An intuitive collage process for self-discovery and community*. Santa Cruz: Hanford Mead.

Gackenbach, J. & Bosveld, J. (1989a). Take control of your dreams. *Psychology Today*, 27–32.

Gackenbach, J. & Bosveld, J. (1989b). *Control your dreams*. New York: Harper and Row.

Gagliardi, J. (2016). *La voie du rêve: Résumé d'une conférence donnée au Congrès de l'International Association for the Study of Dreams (IASD)*, le 7 mai 2016. Retrieved from http://voiedureve.blogspot.ca

Garfield, P. (1999). *La créativité onirique: Du rêve ordinaire au rêve lucide*. Paris: J'ai lu.

Garfield, P. (1997). *The dream messenger: How dreams of the departed bring healing gifts*. New York: Simon and Schuster.

Garfield, P. (1995). *Creative dreaming: Plan and control your dreams to develop creativity, overcome fears, solve problems and create a better self* (2e éd.). New York: Simon and Schuster.

Garfield, P. (1991). *The healing power of dreams*. New York: Simon and Schuster.

Garfield, P. (1990). *Pathway to ecstasy*. New York: Prentice Hall.

Garfield, P. (1988). *Women's bodies: Women's dreams*. New York: Ballantine Books.

Garfield, P. (1987). *Comprendre les rêves de vos enfants*. Paris: Albin Michel.

Garneau, J. & Larivey, M. (2002). *L'auto-développement; psychothérapie dans la vie quotidienne*. Ottawa: Ressources en développement.

Gendlin, E. T. (1986). *Let your body interpret your dreams*. Wilmette, IL: Chiron.

Gendlin, E. T. (1982). *Focusing*. New York: Bantam.

Ginger, S. (2003). *La gestalt, une thérapie de contact* (7e éd.). Paris: Hommes et groupes.

Godard, M. O. (2003). *Rêves et traumatismes ou la longue nuit des rescapés*. Ramonville Saint-Agen: Érès.

Goodbread, J. H. (1987). *The dreambody toolkit: A practical introduction to the philosophy, goals and practice of process-oriented psychology*. New York and London: Routledge and Kegan Paul.

Gordon, D. (2008). *L'éveil spirituel par le rêve: guide pratique de guérison des blessures émotionnelles par le voyage mythique de transformation*. Varennes: AdA.

Gratton, N. (2003). *L'art de rêver*. Québec: Flammarion Québec.

Gratton, N. & Séguin, M. (2014). *Dreams and death: The benefits of dreams before, during and after death*. Kindle Edition.

Gratton, N. & Séguin, M. (2009). *Les rêves en fin de vie: 100 récits de rêves pour faciliter la grande traversée*. Québec: Flammarion Québec.

Hadfield, J. A. (1977). *Dreams and nightmares*. Angleterre: Penguin.

Hall, J. A. (1983). *Jungian dream interpretation*. Toronto: Inner City Books.

Hamel, J. (2021). *Dreams, art therapy and healing: Beyond the looking glass*. New York: Routledge.

Hamel, J. (2017/1993). *Rêves, art-thérapie et guérison: De l'autre côté du miroir*. Montréal: Quebec-Livres.

Hamel, J. (2001). La psychothérapie par l'art: la transformation intérieure par la voie de l'imaginaire. *Revue québécoise de psychologie*, *22*, 33–48.

Hamel, J. (1997). L'approche gestaltiste en thérapie par l'art. *Revue québécoise de Gestalt*, *2*(1), 130–147.

Hamel, J. & Labrèche, J. (2015). *Art-thérapie, mettre des mots sur les maux et des couleurs sur les douleurs: La référence pour comprendre et pratiquer*. Paris: Larousse.

Hampden-Turner, C. (1982). *Maps of the mind*. New York: Collier Books/Macmillan.

Harfield, J. A. (1977/1954). *Dreams and nightmares*. New York: Penguin Books.

Hennevin, E. (2003). Le rêve vu par les neurosciences. *Champ Psychosomatique*, 69–79.

Hill, C. E. (2010). *Working with dreams in therapy: Facilitating exploration, insight and action* (3e éd.). Washington: American Psychological Association.

Hillman, J. (1979). *The dream and the underworld*. New York: Harper and Row.

Hillman, J. & McLean, M. (1997). *Dream*. San Francisco, CA: Chronicle Books.

Hobson, J. A. (1988). *The dreaming brain*. New York: Basic Books.

Hoss, R. J. (2005). *Dream language: Self-understanding through imagery and color: A new approach for personal and professional dreamwork*. Ashland, OR: Innersource.

Hoss, R. J. & Gongloff, R. P. (Eds.). (2017). *Dreams that change our lives*. Asheville, NC: Chiron Publications.

Houde, R. (1986). *Les temps de la vie: Le développement social de l'adulte selon la perspective du cycle de vie*. Montréal: Gaétan Morin.

International Association for the Study of Dreams (IASD). *Dreaming: Journal of the association for the study of dreams*. Washington, DC: Educational Publishing Foundation.

Jacobi, Y. (1965). *The way of individuation*. New York and Toronto: Meridian.

Jobin, A.-M. (2021). *Les portes de la nuit.* Montréal: Édition de l'Homme.

Jobin, A.-M. (2020/2002). *Le nouveau journal créatif.* Montréal: Édition de l'Homme.

Jobin, A.-M. (2017/2013). *Créez la vie qui vous ressemble.* Montréal: Édition de l'Homme.

Jobin, A.-M. (2015). *Fantaisies et gribouillis: 85 Activités créatives pour tous.* Montréal: Le Jour.

Jobin, A.-M. (2012). *Exercices créatifs zen.* Montréal: Le Jour.

Johnson, R. A. (1986). *Inner work: Using dreams and active imagination for personal growth.* San Francisco, CA: Harper and Row.

Jung, C. G. (2001). *Modern man in search of a soul.* Boston, MA: Mariner Books.

Jung, C. G. (1998). *Sur l'interprétation des rêves.* Paris: Albin Michel.

Jung, C. G. (1993). *La guérison psychologique* (6e éd.). Genève: Georg.

Jung, C. G. (1991). *Psyche & symbol.* Edited and with an introduction by Violet S. de Laszlo. New York: Bollingen.

Jung, C. G. (1974). *Dreams.* Princeton, NJ: Princeton University Press.

Jung, C. G. (1972). *Mandala symbolism.* Princeton, NJ: Bollingen Series.

Jung, C. G. (1970). *L'homme à la découverte de son âme.* Genève: Mont-Blanc.

Jung, C. G. (1966). *Ma vie, souvenirs, rêves et pensées.* Paris: Gallimard.

Jung, C. G. (1965). *L'âme et la vie.* Paris: Buchet Castel.

Kabat-Zinn, J. (2009a). *Full catastrophe living: Using the wisdom of your body and mind to face stress, pain, and illness.* New York: Bantam Dell.

Kabat-Zinn, J. (2009b). *Au coeur de la tourmente, la pleine conscience: Guérir du stress, de l'anxiété et de la douleur avec la méditation.* Paris: J'ai lu.

Kalff, D. M. (2004). *Images of the self.* Chicago, IL: Temenos Press.

Kaplan-Williams, S. (1987). *The Jungian-Senoi dreamwork manual: Step-by-step introduction to working with dreams* (13e éd.). Berkeley, CA: Journey Press.

Kellog, R. (2016). *Analyzing children's art.* Girard & Stewart Edition.

Kelzer, K. (1990). *The sun and the shadow, my experience with lucid dreaming.* Virginie: A.R.E. Press.

Krakow, B., Kellner, R., Pathak, D. & Lambert, L. (1996). Long term reductions in nightmares treated with imagery rehearsal. *Behavorial and Cognitive Psychotherapy, 24,* 135–148.

Krakow, B., Sandoval, D., Schrader, R., Keuhne, B., McBride, L., Yau, C. L. & Tandberg, D. (2001). Treatment of chronic nightmares in adjudicated adolescent girls in a residential facility. *Journal of Adolescent Health, 29*(2), 94–100.

Krakow, B. & Zadra, A. (2004). Clinical management of chronic nigthmares: Imagery rehearsal therapy. *Behavioral Sleep Medicine, 1,* 45–70.

Krippner, S. (Ed.). (1990). *Dreamtime and dreamwork: Decoding the language of the night.* Los Angeles, CA: Tarcher.

Laberge, S. (2009). *Lucid dreaming: A concise guide to awakening in your dreams and in your life.* Boulder, CO: Sounds True.

Laberge, S. (2008). *S'éveiller en rêvant: Introduction au rêve lucide.* Paris: Almora.

Laberge, S. (1999). *Le rêve lucide: Le pouvoir de l'éveil et de la conscience dans vos rêves.* Centre de recherche sur le sommeil de l'université Stanford: Oniros.

Laberge, S. (1985). *Lucid dreaming: The power of being awake and aware in your dreams.* New York: Ballantine.

Laberge, S. & Rheingold, H. (1990). *Exploring the world of lucid dreaming.* New York: Ballantine Books.

Lebrun, P. (2015). *La Déesse et la panthère.* Paris: Vega.

Lévesque, A.-M. (2015). L'approche jungienne en art-thérapie. In J. Hamel & J. Labrèche (Eds.), *Art-thérapie, mettre des mots sur les maux et des couleurs sur les douleurs: La référence pour comprendre et pratiquer* (pp. 101–113). Paris: Larousse.

Mattoon, M. A. (1984). *Understanding dreams.* Dallas, TX: Spring Publications.

Mattoon, M. A. (1978). *Applied dream analysis: A Jungian approach.* Washington, DC: V. H. Winston and Sons.

Mc Murray, M. (1988). *The illumination: The healing image.* Berkeley, CA: Wingbow.

McNiff, S. (1992). *Art as medicine.* Boston and London: Shamballa.

Mellick, J. (2001/1996). *The art of dreaming: Tools for creative dream work.* Berkeley, CA: Conari Press.

Mellick, J. (1996). *The natural artistry of dreams: Creative ways to bring the wisdom of dream to waking life.* Berkeley, CA: Conari Press.

Miller, A. (2008a). *The drama of the gifted child: The search for the true self.* New York: Basic Books.

Miller, A. (2008b). *Ta vie enfin sauvée.* Paris: Flammarion.

Miller, A. (2004). *Notre corps ne ment jamais.* Paris: Flammarion.

Miller, A. (1990). *La souffrance muette de l'enfant.* Paris: Aubier.

Miller, A. (1987). *Images d'une enfance.* Paris: Aubier.

Miller, A. (1986). *L'enfant sous terreur.* Paris: Aubier.

Miller, A. (1983). *For your own good: Hidden cruelty in child-rearing and the roots of violence.* Toronto: McGraw Hill.

Mindell, A. (1985). *Working with the dreaming body.* Boston, MA: Routledge and Kegan Paul.

Mindell, A. (1982). *Dreambody: The body's role in relieving the self.* Santa Monica, CA: Sigo.

Morgan, C. A. & Johnson, D. R. (1995). Use of a drawing task in the treatment of nightmares in combat-related post-traumatic stress disorder. *Art therapy, 12*(4), 244–247.

Morley, C. (2013). *Dreams of awakening: Lucid dreaming and mindfulness of dream and sleep.* London: Hay House.

Morris, J. (1985). *The Dream workbook.* New York: Fawcett Crest.

Neu, E. R. (1988). *Dreams and dream groups, messages from the interior.* Berkeley, CA: Corsing Press/Freedom.

Pearce, J. C. (1971). *The crack in the cosmic egg.* New York: Pocket Books.

Perlmutter, D. & Villoldo, A. (2011). *Augmentez la puissance de votre cerveau: La neusoscience de l'illumination.* Varennes: AdA.

Perls, F. S. (1992/1969). *Gestalt therapy verbatim.* Highland, NY: Gestalt Journal.

Perls, F. S. (1972a). *Gestalt therapy verbatim.* Toronto: Bantam.

Perls, F. S. (1972b). *Rêves et existences en gestalt-thérapie.* Paris: Epi.

Perls, F. S. (1970). *"Four lectures" in gestalt therapy now: Theory, techniques, applications.* Palo Alto, CA: Science and Behavior.

Pesant, N. & Zadra, A. (2010). L'utilisation des rêves en psychothérapie: une approche intégrative. *Revue québécoise de psychologie, 31*(2).

Pesant, N. & Zadra, A. (2006). Évaluation de l'utilité clinique de séances d'interprétation du rêve basées sur un modèle cognitif-expérientiel. *Revue québécoise de psychologie, 27*(1), 153–170.

Pesant, N. & Zadra, A. (2004). Working with dreams in therapy: What do we know and what should we do? *Clinical Psychology Review, 24*, 489–512.

Petschek, J. (1981). *The silver bird.* Berkeley, CA: Celestial Arts.

Polster, I. & M. (1983). *La gestalt, nouvelles perspectives théoriques et choix thérapeutiques et éducatifs*. Montréal: Le jour.

Reed, H. (1985). *Getting help from your dreams*. New York: Ballantine Books.

Rhinehart, L. & Engelhorn, F. (1992). Pre-image considerations as a therapeutic process. *The Arts in Psychotherapy, 9*, 55–63.

Rhinehart, L. & Engelhorn, F. (1987). *Sandtray dialogue*. Santa Rosa, CA: Rainbow Bridges.

Rhinehart, L. & Engelhorn, F. (1982). *Notes de cours sur le jeu de sable*. Santa Rosa, CA: Eagle Rock Trail Art Therapy Institute. Traduction libre de l'auteure.

Rhyne, J. (1984). *The gestalt art experience*. Oakland, CA: Magnolia Street Editions.

Rinfret, M. (1992). *Caractéristiques du travail sur le rêve à partir des sons et des mouvements*. Sherbrooke: Unpublished.

Rogers, C. (2003). *On becoming a person: A therapist's view of psychotherapy*. New York: Mariner Books.

Rogers, C. (1968). *Le développement de la personne*. Paris: Dunod.

Rohnnberg, A. & Martin, K. (Éds.). (2011). *Le livre des symboles: Réflexions sur des images archétypales*. Köln: Taschen.

Romey, G. (2005). *Dictionnaire de la symbolique des rêves*. Paris: Albin Michel.

Schwartz-Salant, N. & Murray, S. (1990). *Dreams in analysis*. Wilmette, IL: Chiron.

Sela-Smith, S. (2002). Heuristic research: A review and critique of Moustaka's method. *Journal of Humanistic Psychology, 42*(3), 53–88.

Shafton, A. (1995). *Dream reader: Contemporary approaches to the understanding of dreams*. Albany, NY: State University of New York Press.

Shainberg, C. (2005). *Kabbalah and the power of dreaming: Awakening the visionary life*. Rochester, VT: Inner Traditions.

Sheehy, G. (2006/1976). *Passages: Predictable crises of adult life*. New York: Ballantine Books.

Sheehy, G. (1997/1982). *Pathfinders: Overcoming the crises of adult life and finding our path to wellbeing*. New York: William Morrow and Co.

Sheehy, G. (1982). *Franchir les obstacles de la vie*. Paris: Pierre Belfond.

Sheehy, G. (1977). *Passages: Les crises prévisibles de l'âge adulte*. Paris: Pierre Belfond.

Sher, E. (1978). *A child's library of dreams*. Berkeley, CA: Celestial Arts.

Signell, K. A. (1990). *Wisdom of the heart: Working with women's dreams*. New York: Bantam Books.

Simard, V. & Nielsen, T. A. (2009). Adaptation of imagery rehearsal therapy for nightmares in children: A brief report. *Psychotherapy: Theory, Research, Practice, Training, 46*(4), 492–497.

Singer, C. (1990). *Les âges de la vie*. Paris: Albin Michel.

Sparrow, G. S. (1982). *Lucid dreaming: Dawning of the clear light* (2e éd.). Virginie: A.R.E. Press.

Stein, M. (2009). Symbol as psychic transformer. *Symbolic Life, A Journal of Archetype and Culture, 82*, 1–11.

Tart, C. T. (1990). *Altered states of consciousness*. New York: HarperCollins.

Tart, C. T. (1986). *Waking up, overcoming the obstacles to human potential*. Boston, MA: New Science Library.

Taylor, C. L. (1991). *The inner child workbook: What to do with your past when it won't just go away*. New York: Tarcher Perigee.

Taylor, J. (1992). *Where people fly and water runs uphill: Using dreams to tap the wisdom of the unconscious*. New York: Warner.

Thomas, R. & Michel, C. (1994). 9: Le modèle d'Erikson. In R. Thomas & C. Michel (Dir.), *Théories du développement de l'enfant: Études comparatives* (pp. 241–262). Louvain-la-Neuve, Belgique: De Boeck Supérieur.

Tolaas, J. (1990). The puzzle of psychic dreaming. In S. Krippner (Ed.), *Dreamtime and dreamwork: Decoding the language of the night* (pp. 261–270). Los Angeles, CA: Tarcher.

Turner, B. A. (2005). *The handbook of Sandplay therapy*. Cloverdale, CA: Temenos Press.

Ullman, M. & Zimmerman, N. (1979). *Working with dreams: Self-understanding, problem-solving and enriched creativity through dream appreciation*. Los Angeles, CA: Jeremy P. Tarcher.

Vaughan-Lee, L. (1990). *The lover and the serpent: Dreamwork within a Sufi tradition*. Grande-Bretagne: Element Books.

Vedral, J. (2017). *Collage dream writing: Geschichten aus der Tiefe schreiben*. Wien: Verlag punktgenau.

Viens, S. (2015). L'art-thérapie et le travail des rêves. In J. Hamel & J. Labrèche (Eds.), *Art-thérapie, mettre des mots sur les maux et des couleurs sur les douleurs: La référence pour comprendre et pratiquer*. Paris: Larousse.

Villoldo, A. (2018). *Grow a new body using ancient healing secrets*. Retrieved from www.hayhouseworldsummit.com

Villoldo, A. (2009). *Le courage de rêver: Comment les Shamans créent le monde par le rêve*. Varennes: AdA.

Villoldo, A. (2008). *Courageous dreaming: How shamans dream the world into being*. New York: Hay House.

Villoldo, A. (2007). *Les quatre révélations: Sagesse, puissance et grâce des Gardiens de la terre*. Varennes: AdA.

Villoldo, A. (2006a). *The four insights: Wisdom, power and grace of the Earthkeepers*. New York: Hay House.

Villoldo, A. (2006b). *L'âme retrouvée*. Varennes: AdA.

Villoldo, A. (2000). *Shaman, healer, sage: How to heal yourself and others with the energy medicine of the Americas*. Varennes: AdA.

Von Franz, M.-L. (2008). *La voie des rêves*. Ville d'Avray: La fontaine de Pierre.

Von Franz, M.-L. (2006). *Âme et archétypes*. Ville d'Avray: La fontaine de Pierre.

Von Franz, M.-L. (1992). *Rêves d'hier et d'aujourd'hui*. Paris: Albin Michel.

Von Franz, M.-L. (1983). *Alchemical active imagination*. Zurich: Spring Publications.

Waggoner, R. (1973). *Lucid dreaming: Gateway to the inner self*. Needham, MA: Moment Point.

Waggoner, R. & McCready, C. (2015). *Lucid dreaming: Plain and simple: Tips and techniques for insight, creativity and personal growth*. San Francisco, CA: Conary.

Watkins, M. (1984). *Waking dreams*. Zurich: Spring Publications.

Weinrib, E. (1983). *Images of the self: The Sandtray therapy process*. Boston, MA: Sigo.

Whitfield, C. (2016). *L'enfant en soi: découvrir et rétablir notre enfant intérieur*. Boucherville: Béliveau.

Whitfield, C. & Nuckols, C. (1987). *Healing the child within: Discovery and recovery for adult children of dysfunctional families*. Deerfield Beach, FL: Health communications, Inc.

Wilkinson, M. (2006). The dreaming mind-brain: A Jungian perspective. *Journal of Analytical Psychology, 51*, 43–59.

Windsor, J. (1987). *Dreams healing*. New York: Dodd, Mead and Company.

Wolf, F. A. (1994). *The dreaming universe*. New York: Simon and Schuster.

Woodman, M. (1991). *Dreams: Language of the soul*. [Cassette audio]. Boulder, CO: Sounds True Recordings.

Zadra, A. & Pihl, R. O. (1997). Lucid dreaming as a treatment for recurrent nightmares. *Psychotherapy and Psychosomatics*, *65*(1), 50–55.

Websites

www.artsyshark.com/2017/08/08/featured-artist-kim-vergil

www.IASD.com

www.johannehamel.com

www.kimvergil.com

www.lavoiedureve.com

Author Index

Subject Index

Printed in the United States
by Baker & Taylor Publisher Services